❧ *Masterglass* ❧

Jancis Robinson has been writing about wine since her days as restaurant critic for *Isis*. In 1975 she became assistant editor of the wine trade magazine *Wine & Spirit* and then edited it for four years. She started a wine newsletter which was subsequently sold to the Consumers' Association and became *Which? Wine Monthly* which she edited for two years. She was also founder-editor of the annual *Which? Wine Guide*.

She is the author of *The Wine Book* which was published in 1979, and *The Great Wine Book*, a study of the world's top wines, which won the Glenfiddich award for the best book on wine published in 1982.

She has been wine correspondent of the *Sunday Times* since 1980 and has contributed to a wide range of British and foreign publications, including *Harper's & Queen*, *The Times* and the *TLS*.

Jancis Robinson was writer and presenter of 'The Wine Programme', a six-part television series and Britain's first on wine, shown first in 1983. She is a regular radio broadcaster and has lectured frequently on the art of wine tasting.

Jancis Robinson

Masterglass

A practical course in tasting wine

Illustrated by Ian Dicks

Pan Original

Pan Books London and Sydney

First published 1983 by Pan Books Ltd,
Cavaye Place, London SW10 9PG

ISBN 0 330 28097 X

Phototypeset by Input Typesetting Ltd, London
Printed and bound in Great Britain by
Cox & Wyman Ltd, Reading

For Julia

and the two people who did most to keep her so happy while I wrote this.

Contents

There's no such thing as a born taster

Foretaste

A book for the thirsty

This is a book for people who want to know more about wine, but have had the crucial realization that drinking wine is a lot more fun than reading about it. Happily, the practical side of wine appreciation not only has more immediate appeal than arid theory, it is also considerably more important.

It's horribly easy for those of us who earn our living writing and talking about wine to lose sight of the fact that what actually counts is how it *tastes*. The lovely liquid exists not to fill analysis books or justify vintage charts, but to give sensual pleasure. This 'wet' guide to wine is merely an accompaniment to your wine drinking, explaining why different wines taste the way they do, so that by being an informed wine taster (as opposed to an ignorant drinker) you can maximize your enjoyment.

Masterglass constitutes a complete wine course for the thirsty. It tells the story of how wine is made, explains what influence factors as diverse as climate and bottle-size have on the resultant taste, and demonstrates how to get as much pleasure from wine as possible by the practical way you serve and drink it. All this information is given not just with words but reinforced by scores of different practical exercises – most, but not all, involving that important sport, wine tasting. (Other things you'll be asked to do range from tasting toothpaste to drinking wine from a teacup.)

Down the left-hand side of each page is the theory, which you can demonstrate to yourself by following the exercises outlined alongside on the right-hand side.

The exercises in this book equip the interested wine drinker with all the important explanations of why each wine tastes the way it does. Every taste-shaping factor is illustrated by specific examples, and everyone who completes the exercises should have an extremely good grasp of the fundamentals of wine in its most relevant, but often overlooked, context – in your glass. You can literally taste your way to wine expertise.

Halfway through the course, you should be able to tell a claret from a Burgundy and, by the end, a Rioja from a Rhône and a Mâcon from a Muscadet; making mistakes no more often than the wine professional – that is, no more than half the time.

The course starts with an outline of the personal tasting mechanism and highlights some surprising facts which may well help you get more out of everything you taste – food as well as wine.

This is followed by a detailed look at all sorts of practical aspects of serving and drinking wine. However, the main body of the book is the story of wine told by the painless method of tasting it. There are all sorts of different factors that influence the flavour of a wine, from what goes on fifteen feet below the vineyard to whether the cellar door was left open when the wine was bottled. But the single most important and recognizable factor is the predominant grape variety. For this reason, and because an increasing proportion of the world's wines are now labelled as *varietals* (Cabernet Sauvignon, Chardonnay, Riesling) as opposed to *generics* (Claret, Burgundy, Hock), the main part of the book is divided into sections on each of the major grape varieties.

Initially, this is simply to establish each variety's identity on the palate. A Sauvignon de Touraine and a Sancerre, for instance, are both examples of the same grape variety, and tasting each (plus a dry white Bordeaux and a Fumé Blanc from California) will help form a 'palate picture' of the Sauvignon Blanc grape. Grafted on to each section, however, is a set of increasingly complex and interrelated factors. After you've established what Sauvignon tastes like, for example, you are encouraged to taste examples made in very different climates, so that you can see how fifty per cent more sunshine in a bottle actually *tastes*.

At the end of the book there are also some demonstrations of why some wine and food combinations don't work (though no dogma about which do), some suggestions for further wine-tasting exercises and a short dictionary of the jargon.

How to use this guide

If you want to learn about wine in the speediest and most systematic way that *Masterglass* can offer, you should try to follow the exercises in the order suggested by the course, as this constitutes a logical and precise way of building up your knowledge. There's no reason, however, why you should allow me to dictate your wine-drinking habits. You could perfectly easily allow the wine you happen to be drinking to dictate the order in which you tackle this book. Simply look up the wine you're tasting in the index and find out which exercise(s) it could be useful for.

Certainly, Chapters 3 and 4, on white and red wines respectively, can be tackled in tandem; though even the most free-range wine taster is advised to look first at the two chapters on 'How to taste' and 'Practical matters'.

You can learn a great deal by studying only one wine but, as shown on this course, you can learn at least five times as much by tasting two and comparing them. This means that you could accelerate your progress through this course by getting together with others also interested in finding out more about wine, or by learning how to cope with wine leftovers, or by dramatically increasing your wine consumption. You, your liver and your bank balance will determine which of the two latter possibilities are more sensible, but if you choose the first bear in mind that a normal 75 cl bottle can supply either six good glasses of wine for drinking or up to twenty samples for tasting.

In each exercise, examples of wines suitable for tasting have been described as specifically as is both necessary and possible. Many of the bottles suggested are widely available. For more obscure bottles, specific guidance on how to track them down has been given – which is why the text is littered with wine merchants' names and addresses, correct at the time of writing and supplied with apologies for the fact that the 'winescape' will change during the currency of this book. I have tried to keep the cost of this course down. Some of the bottles specified will sell for little more than £2, and I have suggested bottles costing more than £5 only if they are absolutely necessary to prove a point. It is true, however, that, to some extent, the less you're prepared to spend per bottle, the more slowly you will learn. A Vouvray costing £2.50 a bottle is unlikely to demonstrate the character of the Chenin Blanc grape nearly as effectively as one at £4.

If you really get hooked, you may also want to try some of the more advanced exercises that have been marked 'A-level' which, if done with enthusiasm and at least part of your brain as well as your mouth, will turn you into an informed wine taster.

Why you are Masterglass *material*

No matter how little you know about wine now, you can learn how to taste wine by following this course. It's designed for everyone from the complete novice (nay, teetotaller) upwards. I learnt a great deal myself while compiling it, so I hope that others, who've been exposed to wine for some years, may do so too – especially from Chapters 1 and 2. Those who are relatively new to wine should feel particularly confident, though, since it is they who invariably make the most acute tasters.

The American tasting guru Maynard Amerine points out that the average human adult can detect at least 1,000 different flavours, many of which can be found in wine, so your tasting mechanism is already well equipped to deal with the raw material. All you need is the sort of guidance this course can offer and some confidence. There is no such thing as a born taster. Only a handful of people whose physical disabilities have impaired their senses of taste will find any difficulty at all; and in *blind tasting*, tasting to identify an

For more obscure wines specific guidance has been given on how to track them down

unnamed wine, novices often do better, because their perceptions are unclouded by previous experiences.

This course should turn you into an accomplished 'blind' taster but, perhaps more importantly, shows you how to assess the quality of every wine that comes your way and how to get the most from it.

Despite what some self-styled 'connoisseurs' may suggest, there are no absolutes in wine appreciation. There are some bottles which may, on an objective basis, be technically faulty, but which some tasters may find perfectly enjoyable. There are other famous wines which can count on enough admirers always to command a high price, that most quantifiable of wine measurements, yet they may not appeal at all to some wine drinkers. Never feel that you 'ought' to like or dislike a wine. The most important aspect of any wine is that *you* enjoy it. The aim of this book is to help you enjoy wine more.

1 How to taste

How little we know

It's extraordinary how little we know about something we do as often as eating and drinking. Once food and drink enters our digestive systems there are so many things that can go wrong that the medical profession is well clued up on what goes on there. But surprisingly little is known about the process of tasting that precedes all that, even though we should, in theory, be much more consciously involved in it than in digesting. Presumably, because a malfunctioning gustatory system is not seen as a particularly serious affliction (though it would drive me crazy), medical researchers have not thought it necessary to look very carefully at how we taste. Indeed, Britain's current specialist in the field is attached not to a school of medicine, or even a department of physiology, but to the food science division at Strathclyde University.

Blindfold yourself and get someone to offer you a food that you like, together with one that is similar but slightly different, to see whether or not you can distinguish between them. For example: chocolate cake and plain sponge cake; smoked salmon and smoked mackerel. (Of course they will have to be presented in the same way. If the chocolate has butter icing, then so should the plain sponge cake; and the smoked

If the professionals know remarkably little about how the gustatory system operates in its complex role between mind and body, we ordinary eaters and drinkers understand even less about how to get the most out of the tasting experience. Even those who would claim to appreciate the pleasures of the table (a brave stance in a society where calories are counted and gastronomic pleasures rated so low) have no clear idea how and why they do so. Whether you like chocolate cake, smoked salmon or Beaujolais, your general approach will be to ram as much of it as possible into your digestive system (and therefore *past* your gustatory system) as fast as you can. You vaguely know that by chewing the food you can prolong the pleasure it gives you, and that with wine there's some rather unsavoury gargling business indulged in by professionals. But that, for most of us, constitutes our knowledge of this daily activity.

We may not know much about it, but, as so many of us proudly proclaim, we sure do know what we like. Or do we? We reckon it is the taste of food and drink that we recognize and base our judgements on, but experience shows that when we are left without any clues other than our own sense of taste we can be pretty helpless. By examining carefully how it is that we taste, this wine course should leave the reader considerably better equipped to appreciate wine – and food, for we taste solids and liquids in almost the same way; in fact, physiologically, we can't taste solids until we've transformed them into liquids by chewing them. Experiments show that we can't taste totally dry foods at all, so that a well-blotted tongue would have no chance of telling even that sugar was sweet.

mackerel should be sliced in the same way as the smoked salmon.)

You will need a very cooperative accomplice at this point: either someone who also wants to follow the course, on whom the tables can be turned after you have performed, or someone who loves you a lot and is prepared to indulge this latest idiosyncrasy.

Now if you thought that would be easy, you'll think this next is a cinch. But you'll probably be surprised at how difficult it is to distinguish between a red and a white wine, with you still blindfold and them served at the same temperature, of course. (A blue Bristol glass does the job of the blindfold less conspicuously.)

The odds can be weighted. Whites that taste very 'red' are full bodied and dry. White Burgundy, California Chardonnays, white Rhône wines such as Hermitage Blanc and some of the more traditional white Riojas are obvious examples. Reds that taste 'white' have lots of acidity and not too much weight in the mouth. Friend Beaujolais is a good candidate, as are the north Italian reds Valpolicella and Bardolino and the more elusive reds of the Loire, Chinon and Bourgueil. (Yapp Bros of Mere, Wiltshire, are good on unusual wines from the Loire and Rhône.)

If you want to make things easy for yourself, try to tell the difference between a light, sweetish white such

as a Mosel (the correct German name; for some reason many call it 'Moselle') and a full-bodied, none-too-acid red such as Châteauneuf-du-Pape. Even then, you will probably be surprised to find you have to think twice before pronouncing; and if you try the experiment simply on a red and white French 'vin de table', your local's house wines for example, you'll probably have to think very hard indeed.

The importance of the nose

We tend to think that just as food and drink have a 'look' that is registered by the eyes, they have a 'smell' that is detected by the nose and a 'taste' that is sensed by the mouth. In fact, the line of distinction between the second two is very blurred. If you have a cold and your nose is blocked up, just think how little taste everything seems to have. When you smell something cooking in the oven, don't you feel as though you already know how it's going to taste? If you want to judge whether you'd enjoy the taste of a soup someone is offering you, you smell it.

What we call the 'taste' of something is the composite impression it makes on our minds by what we sense through our noses and our mouths. But, as suggested above, our noses are in fact more sensitive than our mouths. Without our sense of smell we find we are unable to appreciate foods or distinguish between them easily. 'Flavour' is a less misleading term than 'taste', which we tend to think of as necessarily connected with our mouths.

Next time you are eating, try tasting a mouthful with your nose pinched tight shut. Notice how much the flavour of the food changes. If your mouth is shut too, the food is left in a chamber that's enclosed except for the passage at the back of the mouth – and it starts to taste much cruder. A bit of pineapple, for instance, tastes like something that's juicy, sweet and tart, but without the distinctive pineappleness that the nose usually picks up. A spoonful of soup tastes wet and a bit salty, but the flavour isn't nearly as intense as it is when allowed to steam up your nostrils.

Get someone (who will promise not to laugh) to blindfold you and put some sort of nose-clamp on you, whether it be fingers, a clothes-peg or a bulldog clip. Choose three similarly textured but differently flavoured foods, such as grated apple, potato and carrot, and see whether you can distinguish a mouthful of each. If you fail, try adding a really obvious one like grated onion. But don't despair if even the bulb eludes you; it has baffled physiologists' human guinea-pigs before.

There are two aspects of a substance that can carry a message to our brains: what is tangible, the liquid or solid that comes into contact with our tongue and the inside of our mouth, and what is vaporized, the usually invisible gas that is given off by the substance. When we're consciously smelling something, it's this vapour that travels up our nose to the olfactory receptors at the top. When we're chewing the same thing, the vapour travels from the back of our mouths, up what's called the retro-nasal passage, to the same sensory organ. So what we think of as 'tasting' actually includes quite a bit of unconscious 'smelling', and what we call the 'taste' of something necessarily includes a bit of the 'smell'.

NB. When not actually ingesting, do keep your mouth closed during the two experiments outlined above. If you draw in air over the food you're chewing, it will encourage the vapour given off to travel up the retro-nasal passage and give the same sort of messages as the nose would. Notice, too, that as you chew, you break the food down into a mush that you move towards the back of your mouth. It is from there, if your nostrils aren't blocked, that you 'sniff up' the vapour to the olfactory centre.

Although it's difficult for us to do controlled experiments, because we can't shut off the retro-nasal passage, it seems fairly certain that the messages which solids and liquids are able to convey are much less subtle than those wafted up in vapour. This is because our sensing equipment for vapour is capable of much finer distinctions than that for solids and liquids, the tongue and inside of the mouth. By cutting off our sense of smell as much as possible, and simply chewing, we're left with a much less complex impression of the flavour of something than if we don't have it in our mouths at all, but simply smell it – provided, of course, that it's the sort of substance that does give off some sort of vapour.

Different substances vary tremendously in the amount of vapour they have to give. If they are very volatile, and have lots of little

Basic granulated sugar is not very volatile. Take a sniff of the sugar bowl. You get a sort of 'flat' smell at best, but even that is straining the

flavour elements shooting off into the atmosphere all the time, then smelling them will be a interesting and rewarding experience. Wine is very volatile compared, say, to its biblical partner, bread. You don't get nearly as much vapour from a slice of bread as from a glass of wine – though there's a lot of vapour from freshly baked bread straight out of the oven, because the heat has encouraged all the flavour elements to vaporize. Think how much more flavour soup seems to have hot than when it has been allowed to cool. A bowl of cooled soup is not very volatile and therefore not very appetizing, whereas a bowl of hot, volatile soup can be wonderfully enticing, because of its intriguing mesh of messages carried to your olfactory receptors by the vapour. The messages conveyed to the brain by the nose are not necessarily stronger than those conveyed by the mouth, but they are more subtle. Wine is one of the most subtle substances we will ever taste, and one that is naturally volatile and doesn't need to be heated up to give off a vapour full of flavour.

It makes sense therefore to smell a wine every time you drink it.

More detail is given on page 43 about the vital business of wine smelling (so important it has been graced with the dignified title *nosing*), but it is useful first to see how much information about a wine you can get from your mouth.

As demonstrated by the sugar exercise above, we can get very strong sensations from our tongue. Almost all of what we call our taste

imagination. Basically, sugar doesn't smell. It has no easily discernible effect on your nostrils, but it will have a major impact on your (unblotted!) tongue and the inside of your mouth once you have a spoonful of it in there. This is nothing subtle. No great nuances of flavour here, but a coating of the tongue with a great wham of what you know as 'sweetness' and a sort of grating brought about by its coarse, grainy texture. These sensations are a good example of the two possible ways a food or drink can have an impact on us when inside the mouth: respectively by taste or by texture. We look at texture later.

buds (of which we have about 5,000) are located on the tongue, each of them particularly well tuned to one of the basic elements of taste. Physiologists have identified at least four – sweetness, sourness, saltiness and bitterness – and continue to argue about others, which might include oiliness, alkalinity, fattiness and 'metallic-ness'. The first four comprise a very useful model, and different areas of the tongue are supposed to be particularly sensitive to each of them. Of course, individuals vary in their own sensitivities, and you will be able to identify exactly where on your tongue you are most sensitive to each. It is also, therefore, important to try to 'rinse' as much of your tongue as possible with everything you taste. To paraphrase: take a good mouthful.

Capturing the flavour

Sweetness in wine

In very general terms, the highest concentration of those taste buds particularly aware of sweetness is around the tip of the tongue. Perhaps this is why we need only a tiny lick of ice cream to know how sweet it is.

Grape juice becomes wine when yeasts act on the sugar in ripe grapes to convert some, or nearly all, of it (in a way too complicated for most of us to even contemplate) into alcohol. The resulting liquid is therefore drier and stronger than grape juice, but the amount of sweetness left in the finished wine – the residual sugar – varies

Experiment with sugar granules to see where on your tongue you experience sweetness best. Then try with whatever liquids you drink to see if you can assess their sweetness by their impact on your tongue. Now try the same procedure with every wine that comes your way.

Take conscious note of the amount of sweetness you detect in every wine you drink. The following are good examples for each category.

★ *Bone dry: Muscadet; Loire wines based on the Sauvignon grape such as Sancerre, Pouilly-Fumé and Sauvignon de Touraine; most Champagne and other* enormously. Wine can be extra dry, dry, medium dry, medium sweet, sweet and very sweet; though even wines we normally label 'bone dry', because they seem to have no sweetness at all, contain a tiny amount of residual sugar. Sugar content ranges from about 1 to 200+ grams per litre, with dry wines usually having less than 10 grams.

There is no legislation, or even a code of practice, correlating residual sugar content and wine description. For instance, because of the extra marketing cachet in the word 'dry' at the moment, you will find some wines that most experienced tasters would call medium dry being labelled dry, and others that perhaps should be called medium sweet being labelled medium dry. In recent years the mass market has been schooled to feel proud of liking something dry, though now there are instances of inverse snobbery in people such as myself, who perhaps make a bit more noise about liking Asti Spumante and Sauternes than we would if they were more generally liked.

Take a note of the amount of sweetness you detect in every wine you drink

sparkling wines labelled 'brut' (though it's a fallacy that these are 'slimming'); Chablis, although some very ripe years such as 1978 and 1976 will produce wines that are just 'dry'; Germany's 'trocken' wines.

★ *Dry (the biggest category by far, though even within it there are variations – all white Burgundy can be described as 'dry', though wines such as Montagny and Rully tend to be drier than a great Montrachet or Meursault): Loire wines labelled 'sec' and based on the Chenin Blanc grape, such as Vouvray and Saumur; most Alsace wines; white Rhône and Provence wines such as Hermitage Blanc or Coteaux d'Aix-en-Provence Blanc; most white Bordeaux labelled 'sec' or in a green glass bottle; most white 'vin de table' labelled 'sec' or 'dry'; Soave, Verdicchio, Pinot Grigio, Pinot Bianco and most white 'vino da tavola'; white Rioja; most whites from around the Mediterranean such as those from Greece and Cyprus; California's Fumé Blanc and (just) Chardonnay; Germany's 'halbtrocken' wines and some of her lightest 'Kabinett' wines.*

★ *Medium dry: most French wines labelled 'demi sec', especially Vouvrays, and Coteaux du Layon; Gewürztraminer from Alsace; richer Graves; Frascati; most basic white wine made in California, Australia, South Africa and New Zealand, plus Chenin Blanc, Steen, Semillon and Müller-Thurgau ('Riesling-Sylvaner') made there; the great majority of German wine sold in Britain, including most*

Bordeaux shape ***Burgundy shape***

We tend to think that it's only white wines that vary in sweetness. Rosés do as well, of course, with Provence being responsible for good examples of bone-dry pink wines and most Rosé d'Anjou being medium dry to medium sweet. But it is perhaps more of a revelation to examine the varying degrees of sweetness in red wines. Port is the supreme example of a very sweet red, but it is a wine that has been *fortified* by the addition of extra alcohol – other popular examples of fortified wines being Sherry, Vermouth and to a lesser extent Madeira and Marsala.

'Tafelwein' and 'Qualitätswein' (which includes Liebfraumilch).

★ *Medium sweet: most French wines labelled 'moelleux'; 'vendange tardive' wines from Alsace; Asti Spumante and Moscato Spumante; Moscatel de Setubal; commercial Tokay from Hungary; Rhine Auslese and Mosel Beerenauslese.*

★ *Sweet: Sauternes and Barsac; most Muscats such as the popular one from Beaumes de Venise; Rhine Beerenauslesen and Mosel Trockenbeerenauslesen.*

★ *Very sweet: Sauternes in a year like 1976; Rhine 'TBA'; a host of fortified wines.*

Vinho Verde varies tremendously in sweetness because some brands are specially sweetened (to differing degrees) for export. Compare different specimens of these inexpensive Portuguese whites, noting for instance that the best-known Aveleda is on the cusp of medium dry and medium sweet, whereas Casal Mendes, Verdegar and Magrico are tooth-tinglingly dry.

Try some of these to see how sweetness can vary in red wines, though admittedly about 85 per cent of all reds can be described as 'dry'.

★ *Bone dry: red Loires such as Bourgueil, Chinon and Saumur Rouge (Peter Dominic stock one); Italy's 'high altitude' wines such as Barolo, Barbaresco and Brunello di Montalcino.*

★ *Medium dry: California's Cabernet Sauvignon, much Zinfandel; Châteauneuf-du-Pape; Lambrusco; many Tyrolean reds; Australian Shiraz;*

Ordinary unfortified wines are known in EEC parlance as 'light wines' (we can no longer use the term 'table wines' because they have nabbed this for everyday, basic-level-of-quality wine) and even light red wines can be anything from bone dry to medium sweet.

Hirondelle red table wine; Paul Masson California Carafe Red.

★ *Medium sweet: California's late harvest Zinfandels; some of South Africa's beefier reds.*

Most very cheap wines and many very popular ones have quite a lot of residual sugar because, respectively, sweetness can mask many a rough edge and it is a very easy taste to appreciate.

Acidity – the vital spark

Sweetness (or lack of it, i.e. dryness) may be the most obvious of the four basic tastes to students of wine, but what physiologists call sourness is the most vital to the wine itself. Sourness is a measure of acidity, of which there's a lot in lemon juice and vinegar and little or none in flour and water. The upper edges of the tongue (towards the back of the mouth for me) are most sensitive to acidity.

Take a smell of something high in acidity. Vinegar of any sort is fine (lemon juice is not as volatile). Notice how the edges of your tongue curl up in anticipation of the experience of how it would taste in your mouth. Acidity has such a strong effect on the tongue, it is the easiest of the four basic tastes to imagine, without any liquid or solid stimulus at all. But if you really want to prove the point to yourself, sip some lemon juice or vinegar. Whether imagining, smelling or sipping, notice which part of your tongue reacts most strongly to acidity.

Too much acidity makes something sour; just enough enlivens it, giving it appealing 'zip' or a crisp tartness. Sweetness and acidity are closely interrelated. As a fruit ripens, it gets sweeter and sweeter while losing acidity. An over-ripe pear, for instance, is bland and unappetizing because it has so much less acidity than one picked at just the right moment.

Now start smelling every drink you take, whether it's alcoholic or not. Notice that most drinks do actually have some sort of refreshing acidity in them. Still water won't make your tongue crinkle – it marks the frontier between acid and alkaline – but all fruit juices, carbonated drinks, milk, and even tea and coffee have some sort of tingling effect on the tongue. Notice too how important a

Getting the balance between sweetness and acidity right in wine grapes is crucial. The winemaker wants his grapes to be as ripe as possible for two reasons. Firstly, the longer they're on the vine the more interesting flavours they will have had time to develop; and, secondly, the sweeter the grape juice the sweeter and/or stronger the resultant wine will be, strength being seen as a tantalizing commodity in wine regions far from the equator. He mustn't, on the other hand, leave the grapes on the vine so long that the acidity falls to a level that will make the wine bland (nor so long that they will be ruined by hail, rain or frost). And, for white wines designed to live long, acidity acts as a sort of embalming fluid.

There are many different acids in wine, the most common being tartaric; indeed, scrapings from wine vats are the chief ingredient in commercially available 'cream of tartar' preparations. The embryonic wine taster need not worry if he is unable to distinguish between, say, gluconic and glyconic acids; all you need be concerned about is the general level of acidity as it appears to your senses. The acidity level may be high for several reasons: the wine was made from grapes grown where ripening sunshine has been at a premium (either because of distance from the equator or altitude of the vineyard); the grapes were picked before they were fully ripe; there was not enough sunshine in that particular year to ripen the grapes fully; or acidity has been added chemically to the wine or must (the fermenting grape juice). This practice is allowed in a surprising range of

component acidity is in fruit; lemons, grapefruit, gooseberries and blackcurrants are all common examples of fruits with so much natural acid that most of us have to add sweetness before we can eat them. Monitor the different tastes in a batch of fast-evolving fruits, such as pears or tomatoes, as they lose acidity and start to taste dull.

Start registering acid levels as you taste wine

If you have some cream of tartar in the house, make up a solution of it and add it in varying amounts to an ordinary table wine. (Heaven forbid such desecration of anything smart.) If you choose a fairly sweet wine, a cheap Portuguese or Spanish white for example, you might even be able to 'correct' it to a more acceptable level of acidity.

To get a very, very crude idea of the flavours of different sorts of acidity found in wine, familiarize yourself with these:

tartaric acid – cream of tartar in solution
malic acid – apple juice
citric acid – lemon, grapefruit or orange juice
lactic acid – milk or yogurt
acetic acid – vinegar
carbonic acid – fizzy drinks

countries and, when done carefully and undetectably to the taster, can often make for a better end-result.

The delicate balance between sweetness and acidity in ripe grapes is reflected in the resulting wines. The sweeter the wine, the more acidity is needed to stop it being cloying. The most obvious difference between a poor and a great Sauternes is the amount of acidity there is to counterbalance all that sugar.

At the other end of the spectrum, a very dry wine doesn't need all that much acidity to make it appetizing and crisp. A bone-dry wine that had as much acidity as a Sauternes would be mouth-puckeringly tart. The acidity of wine tends to be between 3 and 9 grams per litre.

Next time you decide to treat yourself to the taste of a good Sauternes, which in general means a classed growth with the words 'cru classé' on the label, and costing upwards of £6 a bottle, spend another £3 on a bottle labelled simply 'Sauternes' or 'Barsac'. (All Barsac is Sauternes, but not all Sauternes is Barsac; such is the law governing the use of the names of these two villages near Bordeaux.) You can use the remains of the cheaper wine for cooking a poulet sauterneais perhaps, or, better still, use the Grants of St James's generic Sauternes as your example of uninspiring sweet wine – available in half-bottles for about £2 from Victoria Wine.

Getting the balance between sugar and acidity right is an important part of winemaking. Wines that are too high in acidity right from the start are called *green*. (Other sorts of acids may develop and become apparent to the taster at specific points in the wine's life, but this is A-level stuff and discussed on page 35.) There is nothing sacred or technical about the term 'green', of course; it just happens to be an adjective commonly used for over-acid wines. *Tart* is another word used for the phenomenon, though more often for whites than reds. Noticeable but not overwhelming acidity is a very desirable quality in white wines, for we expect them to refresh us, whereas most red wines are expected to provide more nourishment and a bit of intrigue. Whites with marked,

Start registering acidity levels as you taste wine. The following are some possible examples of wines at each extreme:

★ *Green or tart: Gros Plant Nantais from the Loire; Coteaux Champenois (the still wines of Champagne; I always think they demonstrate perfectly why Champagne should have bubbles in it); many English wines; Luxembourg's wines; 1977 Claret; 1977, 1975 and some 1981 red Burgundy; Vinho Verde from Portugal; Valdeorras from Spain (just across the border from Vinho Verde country).*

★ *Crisp: almost all Loire wines, no matter how sweet they are; Mosel wines; Chablis and lots of other white Burgundy; lots of other* but not unpleasant, acidity are often called *crisp*. 'Hmm, nice and crisp,' a taster might mutter appreciatively over a white wine feared to be a little low on acidity because it was grown somewhere quite hot. Wines, both red and white, that have rather too little acidity are often called *flabby*, one of those words that gets wine tasting a bad name. Yes, it does sound a bit ridiculous. If you can't bear to use it, you could use 'flat' instead. A flat or flabby wine is merely dull because it lacks sufficient acidity to enliven it. A *cloying* wine is one that is really sweet and doesn't contain enough acidity to balance the sweetness.

well-made whites from slightly warmer regions.

★ *Flabby or flat: much more difficult to generalize here as it depends on individual winemakers' skills, but many North African and other wines, red and white, made close to Mediterranean shores tend to flab. You will sense a sort of drabness in the overall impact of the wine and find yourself still looking for the 'lift' of a bit of acidity as the wine goes through the mouth.*

★ *Cloying or too sweet: cheap very sweet wines of all sorts, either sweet white Bordeaux such as poor quality Sauternes or Barsac or the sweetest representatives in a range of branded wines such as Rocamar (Arthur Cooper), Don Cortez (Victoria Wine) or Justina (Peter Dominic).*

It can be devilishly easy to confuse acidity and dryness. A lot of us think we're drinking a very dry wine because it seems like hard work, when in fact it may simply be too high in acidity. Because a little sweetness is useful to mask none-too-brilliant winemaking, it's a favourite trick of the blenders of cheap 'dry' whites to market a medium dry wine with a massive dollop of acid in it to keep the fans happy.

Now try the 'dry white' in such a range – perhaps a glass of dry white at your local pub – and see if, by carefully registering how your tongue reacts, you can sort out the sweetness from the acidity.

The other basic tastes

Saltiness is a basic taste that is vitally important in food but rarely found in wine. One of the wonderful old chestnuts of wine lore is that the difference between a Fino and a

Make up a saline solution by dissolving some salt in water and swill it about your mouth, noticing which bits of the tongue react most strongly. I find it is the part just in

Manzanilla Sherry is that Manzanilla acquires a salty tang because it's matured on the coast at Sanlucar de Barrameda instead of inland at Jerez. One has only to consider for a moment that the town also produces a Fino, and that the other 'Sherry port' Puerto de Santa Maria does not produce a Manzanilla, to smell something fishy rather than salty. In fact both Fino and Manzanilla can be slightly salty, and I have even tasted a trace of sàltiness in some white wines from New Zealand, but such perceptible saline intrusions into the world of wine are exceptional. The description of the saltiness-tasting mechanism is included here more for comprehensiveness than for usefulness in wine tasting.

from the ultra-acid-conscious edges at the back, and bits of the front edges too. Next time you want to check the seasoning in some savoury dish, make sure this part of your tongue is exposed to your sample of it. Next time you smell or taste a Fino or Manzanilla Sherry – the very dry light ones, Tio Pepe and La Ina, are good examples – notice how the salt-sensitive parts of your tongue react.

Make up saline solution

The fourth and final basic taste that the tongue is capable of registering is bitterness, to which the flat back part of the tongue is particularly sensitive. Like saltiness, bitterness is much less important to wine tasters than sweetness and acidity, but quite a number of Italian reds leave a bitter taste at the back of the tongue.

So now your tongue should be fully trained to do its damnedest with any wine (and, more importantly, food) that comes its way. You should be able to assess the sweetness and acidity of any substance – as well as its saltiness and bitterness if necessary. You may be glad to hear that you now have a scientific excuse to take your wine in fairly large mouthfuls, for you should expose all of your tongue to the liquid.

To isolate bitterness, you could try putting a few drops of bitters such as Fernet Branca, Underberg, Angostura or Suze in some water and rinsing that round your mouth, noticing a flat, rasping sensation on the back part of your tongue. Campari is another very bitter liquid, but it is also very sweet – an interesting tasting exercise in itself. See how it needs the acidity of soda water (carbonic acid) and/or a slice of lemon or orange (citric acid) to make it a refreshing drink. The Italians obviously have a certain monopoly on bitterness. Assess each Italian red you taste for it. Some of the most renowned – Brunello, Vino Nobile di Montalcino and lots of Piedmont reds, such as Barolo – have some degree of bitterness, but then so do many examples of the much lighter

Of course, you won't always carefully identify each basic taste separately. The wine makes a composite impression on your senses as you swill it about your mouth, but sweetness and acidity are crucial to that overall impression.

and more humble Valpolicella and Bardolino.

More crude feelings

You can learn a bit more than the simple sensations of sweetness, acidity, saltiness and bitterness by the tangible effect of a wine on your tongue and insides of the mouth. One of the most obvious, and sometimes even pain-producing ingredients in many red wines is *tannin*. This is a convenient shorthand term for all sorts of tannins or polyphenols that either find their way into a wine from the grape skins, stems and pips or develop as a result of the wood in which the wine has been stored – or sometimes both.

Allow tea to stew in a pot and take a mouthful

In ordinary eating and drinking, tannin is most noticeable in tea, particularly when it has been allowed to stand and lots of tannin has been extracted from the leaves. [That thin skin on walnuts is a good example of tannin too.] The sensation that tannin produces in the mouth is perhaps even more crude than any we have studied so far. The insides of the mouth and the gums seem to pucker up in a pretty nasty way when confronted by noticeable tannin: one reason why tasting young red wines that are destined for great things can be hard work.

Allow some tea to stew in the pot and then take a mouthful, without any milk to soften the impact of this ungenerous liquid. Notice how you react. There's a bit of acidity there, perhaps a trace of bitterness too, but there's also something quite different from either of these components that is so distasteful it almost makes you want to screw up your eyes. This is tannin, and I feel the puckering sensation strongest between my gums and the insides of my cheeks. Notice where it affects you most, as it will depend on how you drink. Some people notice it particularly on the roof of the mouth.

Wines don't contain tannin to taste good now, but in the hope that they'll taste good in the future. Just as white wines to be kept need acidity in their youth, tannin acts as a sort of preservative to prolong the active life of a great red wine. Wine is capable of absorbing all sorts of tiny flavour elements when it is young, but needs time for these to knit together to produce a complex, mature wine. The tannins themselves break down and combine with other elements to contribute towards this ideal. One of the skills of the winemaker is to judge just how much tannin is needed at the beginning to balance the other flavour elements, most of them from the grape, as they evolve. Red Bordeaux or Claret provide the best examples of this. These are wines many vintages of which are capable of achieving venerable and gracious old age, which will be all the more gracious if they contain a fair amount of tannin at the outset. A tasting of young, good quality Clarets, under three years old, say, can be a great strain. The tannin content is so high that it puckers the mouth immediately, leaving the senses straining to detect some indication of fruit. Very few people are sufficiently experienced and masochistic to judge wines of this sort. *Hard* is the word used to describe a wine that has too much tannin.

As the wines mature, the tannins become less evident and the taste seems much *softer*. The fruit-based flavours at last start to emerge in subtle and complex formations. Ideally, the tannin will finally fade to insignificance as the wine's flavour

Now try to assess every red wine you drink for its tannic impact on your mouth. Somewhat ironically, most examples of over-tannic wines cost rather a lot because, although they're youthful, they are rather smart. For a textbook example of good wine at this early, unfriendly stage, you will have to spend at least £6 on a bottle of good Claret from a Médoc village such as St Estèphe, Pauillac or St Julien, and a vintage such as 1982, 1981 or 1978. A bottle of wine from the same château but from the 1979 or 1976 vintage would admirably prove the point about the contrastingly soft allure of wines made from less tannic grapes. And a bottle from a much older, good vintage – 1971 or 1970 perhaps – would show how lovely a wine can be once the tannin has retreated into the background and allowed the fruit and oak flavours to marry and produce many different nuances. Some mature Portuguese reds are hard because they have been left in wood too long, and can provide the tannic experience cheaply.
Most other inexpensive wines won't have much tannin. This is due in part to their not being made from the aristocratic grape varieties that tend to give tannic wines, but also because no one would dream of treating them to the new, small oak casks in which great Clarets are aged. There are, however, many moderately priced examples of 'soft' young wines.

Tannin is not an important constituent of Beaujolais, for example, and nor is it in most Riojas. The wines of north-eastern Italy, as well as Merlot and Cabernet, are also soft, and even Bordeaux is producing some low-tannin wines based on the

reaches its peak of maturity (though of course no one knows when this peak has been reached until it's been passed). Part of wine's great interest is that it is so unpredictable. A vintage that can look good at the outset, so good that winemakers are happy that the wines contain lots of tannin to preserve them for a glorious future, can fail to come up with the luscious goods, and the fruit fades long before the tannin dissipates.

Wines can also have too little tannin, though this doesn't make for unpleasant drinking in the way that over-tannic wines do – it's merely a waste of potential. A wine may have lots of lovely gutsy fruitiness when young, offering immediate attractive soft drinking; but all these flavours would have been capable of maturing into something more magnificent had there been more tannin to preserve them into middle or old age.

Tannin is chiefly an important component of red wines, partly because grape skins, stems and pips don't play an important part in white winemaking (see page 76) and partly because the pigments derived from the skins are needed to interact with the tannins to soften them. Some white wines taste astringent, in the same way as tannic reds, because they have been made from grape juice that has been pressed very hard and roughly out of the grapes, so that they contain a certain amount of tannin from the skins – and probably the pips too.

Different red grape varieties tend to produce wines with different levels

usually tannic Cabernet Sauvignon grape. Belair Claret from Sichel and Pierre Coste wines, available from Adnams of Southwold, are good examples of wines made with such new techniques.

The 1957 vintage in Bordeaux was one of those that simply had too much tannin to give any other flavours a chance. You'll be hard put to find a representative (and why should you, after all?), but try as many 1975s as you can find. There is current debate at the spittoon about whether that vintage won't also turn out to have too much tannin for its own good.

White wines have an astringency of their own. We tend to call whites 'astringent' instead of tannic, but the feeling in the mouth is the same. Next time you taste a cheap Italian white, notice what happens to the most puckerable bit of your mouth. For me, many cheap Soaves produce the same sensation as youthful Clarets.

of tannin. The thicker the skins, the higher the tannin content in the must. Cabernet Sauvignon, Syrah and Nebbiolo grapes are particularly tannic. Vintages when there has been a shortage of rain to swell the flesh of the grapes also tend to produce tannic wines because skins and tannin represent a high proportion of the must.

The addition of tannins is more widespread than people realise

The winemaker can try to extract as much tannin as possible from the grapes by the way he chooses to make the wine. If he encourages a long fermentation and then lets the wine rest in contact with the skins for an extended period after that, called the *cuvaison* in France, there will be ample opportunity for lots of tannin to seep out of the skins and into the wine.

When wine is left in contact with wood it tends to extract what tannins there are in that material. The less an oak cask has been used before, the more tannins there are available. So really great wines that are thought capable of ageing up to perhaps five decades are often put into new casks. Although such casks are much more expensive than used ones, they set the wine up better for a long life.

The longer a wine is left in wood, the more its natural fruitiness will dissipate. Some very traditionally made Barolos are good examples of wines that have been kept so long in wood that the tannin overwhelms every other flavour component.

Whenever a bottle of Barolo from a lesser vintage (1977, 1975, 1973 or indeed any that costs less than £5) comes your way, see what you think is its predominant characteristic. So dry and so drying is such a Barolo, drinking it without food is unthinkable. Only examples from rich, ripe years, such as 1978, 1974, 1971 and 1970, and from good producers, such as Ceretto, Franco-Fiorina, Pio Cesare, Ratti, Cordero and Conterno, and the individual vineyard wines of Fontanafredda, have managed to convince me of Barolo's greatness. Too often, drinking Barolo can be like sucking a matchstick.

Less expensively, the Portuguese reds of the early and mid-1970s, which were a speciality of Oddbins at one time, can demonstrate the same phenomenon. What original fruitiness

There is now drinkable (but sometimes only just) evidence of a wonderful piece of specious logic concerning wine and tannin. A few winemakers in emerging quality wine regions, California in particular, observed that most great red wines started off life with a high tannin content. They seem to have developed this into the notion that wines with a very high tannin content would automatically be thought to be very great. (The chemical addition of tannins in the form of tannic acid is much more widespread than most wine drinkers realize.) One wonders whether the tannic monsters produced in California in the early 1970s will ever, as they say, 'come round' to enjoyable drinkability.

they had has disappeared without trace, leaving in many cases an unpleasantly hard wine.

Look out for bottles of Zinfandel and Cabernet Sauvignon from top California producers. The earlier models are extremely difficult to find and more up-to-date ones can seem fiendishly expensive, but you will find very noticeable tannin in most wines made in the 1970s.

Slimline and fuller-bodied wines

Just like people, wines have a weight – though there is no vinous shame in being full bodied. A wine's weight is a measure of how much extract and alcohol it has. A full-bodied wine has an alcohol content upwards of, say, 12.5 per cent and has lots of flavour. A light wine will probably be less than 10 per cent alcohol and is a much flimsier specimen. It's difficult to describe how you assess weight, but it is actually quite easy to do. Simply by looking at the wine you can get a clue (see page 42) and, with practice, when you smell it you often get quite a strong hint. But it is in the mouth that wine sends its strongest 'guess-the-weight' message: it really is the physical sensation of how heavy the liquid feels in the mouth. When you have

Start taking note of the alcohol content when it's stated on a wine label and relating it to how 'heavy' the wine feels in your mouth. If a wine is very alcoholic, you may well feel like avoiding naked flames when you breathe out. Beware the candles after the Côte Rôtie. Notice particularly the hot, alcoholic sensation you feel on your breath after swallowing a glass of port.

a mouthful of the wine do you feel overwhelmed by the intensity of what's in there, or is it a much more watery liquid? (Water makes up well over 80 per cent of the volume of most wines.)

Fortified wines are all very full bodied because they contain added alcohol. Most of the heaviest non-fortified wines are reds such as the Amarone wines of Italy, Hermitage and Châteauneuf-du-Pape of the Rhône and typical Cabernet Sauvignons from California, Australia and South Africa. Great white Burgundy, Sauternes and, especially, California Chardonnays can, however, be very full indeed. Much alcohol actually tastes rather sweet, which is why many California Chardonnays taste as though they contain more residual sugar than they do.

Take a note of how heavy wine feels in the mouth

If a wine is very alcholic you may well feel like avoiding naked flames

Most German wines are very light bodied; indeed, some are only about 6 per cent alcohol. Vinho Verde, whether white or the rarely exported red, is also light. Beaujolais and a host of southern French reds such as Costières du Gard, Minervois and most *vins de pays* are very light, even though most of us think of all reds as fairly full bodied. Many New Zealand wines are very light.

Examine a glass of everyday German wine alongside one of everyday Spanish. Notice how much more of an imposition on your senses the Spanish one is.

A wine doesn't have to have lots of residual sugar to be full. Great Italians such as Brunello and Barolo can be full but dry, while Asti

Now 'look at' (great wine-trade euphemism for 'taste') the everyday German, making sure it's not a 'trocken' or 'halbtrocken' – our old

Spumante is sweet but light. If you're watching your weight, go for wines that are both light and dry. Perhaps this is what accounts for the popularity of Muscadet, Sancerre, Chablis and Beaujolais.

friend Liebfraumilch would be fine. By shutting your eyes and concentrating on a mouthful, make sure you can distinguish between the sensations of sweetness and its lack of body.

Try to taste a Barolo and notice how dry yet full bodied it is. Next time you can sip at some Asti Spumante (some are awful, but Asti Martini can usually be relied upon) savour its lightness at the same time as noticing how sweet it is on the tip of your tongue.

Capturing the flavour

If all a wine could tell us was that it was crisp, medium dry, fairly light and slightly astringent, there would be no need for this book, and little pleasure in wine drinking. Wine's great attraction is that, more than any other drink, it is capable of an amazing variety of flavour – particularly when one considers that there is only one raw ingredient. (Imagine smart societies devoted to tasting different vintages of fermented carrot juice, or specialist gourmet tours of banana warehouses.)

As we have seen, the taste buds alone are capable of receiving only the fairly crude messages that the liquid wine can transmit. The really interesting bit, the wine's identity that we call its flavour, is carried by the volatile elements – up through the nose when we sniff and up from the back of the mouth when we taste – to the olfactory centre, the ultra-sensitive mechanism that deals with flavour. The *vapour* of the wine consists of the volatile esters and aldehydes that form a tiny but vital proportion of each wine's composition. It is their particular profile that makes up each wine's flavour, and to experience this flavour fully it does, of course, makes sense to get the vapour up to the olfactory centre by smelling or nosing the wine.

Now for the problem: how to describe wine flavour. 'Mmm, delicious' or even 'Uuugh' will do – if you never want to communicate with anyone else about wine; if you see no need to remember anything about specific wines; or if you choose not to enjoy the pleasures of comparison and monitoring that wine can offer. Readers of this book, however, will already have decided that they are interested in tasting wine properly, in order to assess it and to enjoy it more – possibly even with a view to blind tasting. What you will find is how frustrating it is to be confronted by a wide and thrilling range of sensations for which there is no cut-and-dried notation or vocabulary.

Music lovers know perfectly well what is meant by middle C and *fortissimo*. Connoisseurs of the visual arts agree on what's meant by square and (more or less) Cubism. For wine tasters there is no definitive term or mark for something as simple and distinctive as the flavour of the Gamay grape, say; let alone for the nuances it's given by the various other factors that paint the 'palate picture', such as the soil the grapes were grown in, the weather that led up to the harvest and the way the wine was made and stored.

An accepted vocabulary would clearly be very useful for wine tasters, and considerable efforts are being made to agree on one. The most respected attempt on this side of the Atlantic is the listing formulated by Michael Broadbent, head of Christie's wine department, in his classic *Wine Tasting*, while Maynard Amerine's much shorter and more rigorous collection in *Wines: Their Sensory Evaluation* provides a reference for American tasters.

But there are curious disparities, even between these two authorities, using the same basic language. The eminent and urbane Broadbent cites *flinty* as 'an evocative overtone. Certain white wine grapes grown on certain soils have a hint of gun-flint in the bouquet and flavour, e.g. Pouilly Blanc Fumé.' Amerine and his colleague Roessler on the other hand dismiss the tasting term with appropriate acidity: 'We confess that this flavor has never come our way. Perhaps *metallic* would do as well. Best to avoid it.' They describe the characteristic scent of Cabernet Sauvignon as *green olive*, while we British tasters are schooled to call it *blackcurrant*. The Australians, that other wine nation divided from us by a common language, are even blunter in their tasting vocabulary. An A-level in chemistry and maths would help you with the problem, but one in English would be a definite disadvantage. And you can doubtless imagine the variance between our tasting terms and those of the French.

Some work has been done by an enterprising Burgundian and, separately, by a hard-working Welshman to come up with definitive *essences* representing in a very concrete and indisputable way exactly what each term 'smells' like. The Burgundian has even marketed a little box of phials so that, as you taste a wine, you can smartly refer to the essence bank to see whether you're right to describe it as 'woody' or as 'violets'.

As these two last examples suggest, choosing words to describe wine is largely a matter of making comparisons with things that are not wine. Earlier parts of this course suggested terms such as 'medium dry,' 'green' and 'soft' which are fairly widely accepted conventions for describing some of wine's more obvious dimensions. When it comes to something as subtle as the wine's flavour, however, things are more difficult. It's a bit like the difference between describing someone's physical attributes (height, complexion and so on) and their character. Tasters tend to look for similarities to other flavours they've experienced or can imagine. Michael Broadbent notes *goaty*, for instance, as 'a rich ripe animal-like flavour. For example, ripe fat Pfalz wines made from the Traminer grape.' I find it hard to imagine him earnestly sniffing a goat preparatory to making this observation; this is merely an accepted term that has evolved.

You can evolve your own wine-tasting vocabulary. If a wine smells like clean sheets to you, then register it. All you need is a term that leads you from a sniff of the wine to a judgement of it. If Michael Broadbent takes a whiff of a ripe fat Rheinpfalz Gewürztraminer, he will say 'Ah, goaty' to himself and come up with an identification of the wine using this trigger word. We all have our own trigger words for various flavours. Throughout the rest of the wine course I will try to suggest a wide range of possible terms for each flavour examined, in the hope that they will help you to develop your own tasting vocabulary. It will be useful, but not essential, if your vocabulary is like that of other people. Non-professionals can make up their own rules for the game of wine tasting – though people in the wine trade who attempt its stiffest test, the Master of Wine examinations, are expected to use commonly accepted terms.

On page 161 there is a glossary suggested of terms to describe the dimensions of a wine, together with words commonly used to recall wine flavours. At this stage it is useful to distinguish between the two words *bouquet* and *aroma*. The first is conventionally used to describe the smellable flavour that has developed during the wine's maturation, while a wine's aroma is directly attributable to the grapes that made it.

Three pointers to quality

Sweetness, acidity, tannin level and body give you the dimensions of a wine. The flavour is the vital clue to its character. But if you want to be able to pick out wines you particularly like, and avoid the mean ones, it's helpful to know about three final aspects of wine that can be judged by the nose and mouth, and which point directly to quality or lack of it.

Effect of lemon juice on the tongue

Cleanliness

The first of these is rather negative. A wine is described as *clean* if it has no obvious faults. Your nose is by far the best judge of this. If after the first sniff you feel you still want to go on, then the wine is clean. Here are a few of the most common nasty smells or, in rather more polite American parlance, 'off-odors'.

- ★ Acetic/vinegary/'pricked': a wine that has already started to turn to vinegar and smells like it (Britain's vinegar merchants buy up job lots of acetic wine from the British wine trade).
- ★ Cardboard: this is a very personal one, but I find it a common smell in cheap wines. It probably arises from the wine being treated with less-than-pristine equipment. 'Filter pads,' mutter some tasters darkly.
- ★ Corked/corky: a catch-all term for a wine that is undeniably off. The wine smell is a combination of musty, mould and just plain old 'orrid. In ancient cellars weevils eating their way through corks used to be a common cause. Nowadays the cause is more likely to be a substandard cork the structure of which allows in air and even nastier things. It is generally agreed that the average quality of corks, which come chiefly from Portugal, has fallen.
- ★ Geraniums: this reminiscent whiff is a sign that a wine has been coarsely treated with sorbic acid.
- ★ Oxidized: recognizing this takes a bit of familiarization. Sherry and Madeira are oxidized, i.e.

Leave some not very precious wine standing out in a glass for a couple of days, somewhere you visit regularly such as the kitchen. Every time you pass it, take a sniff and notice how it changes. It gradually loses its fresh, fruity aroma and begins to get stale. Then the flavour goes flat and the wine is distinctly unappetizing. This is oxidized wine. If you leave it out for even longer the wine will eventually turn to vinegar, and along the way it can be described as acetic. The length of time this process of deterioration takes and how great an effect it has on the senses vary tremendously from wine to wine. Fortified wines like Sherry and Madeira deteriorate very slowly indeed. In general terms, the more body a wine has the longer it will last before deteriorating. Some very strongly flavoured 'light' wines can seem more attractive after a day or two of being exposed to air. Some youthful Australian and California reds, as well as some Italians, can benefit from a bit of aeration. (See page 58 for more on air, wine and decanters.)

It would be a waste of your money to buy bottles that might demonstrate wine faults to you. Try befriending a local wine merchant or the manager of the local off-licence, whose eyes should light up when you say you're taking a wine course; capitalize on this and ask for any bottles that are returned because of a fault – well, 'suspected fault' might be a more tactful way of putting it. There is no shame in a corked bottle. It's not a sign of poor winemaking, exposed to oxygen, something which is usually deliberately avoided in winemaking. Oxidation is a fault in light wines and makes them taste/smell flat and stale. 'Madeirized' is almost synonomous, but used chiefly for white wines.

★ Pear drops: the smell of acetate is quite common in young Beaujolais. Not a very serious fault, unless you hate pear drops.
★ Rotten eggs/mercaptan: this is the smell associated with hydrogen sulphide or H_2S and comes about when sulphur, the winemaker's invaluable antiseptic, has combined with other elements in the wine. Australian noses seem particularly susceptible to mercaptan.
★ Sulphury: this smell of sulphur dioxide or SO_2, like a recently struck match or a solid fuel stove, sometimes lingers over wines that were treated to too much sulphur at some point and is common in cheap sweet whites. It will disappear if you swirl the wine around in the glass.
★ Volatile acidity: the whisper 'VA' goes up occasionally in the tasting room when a wine is obviously unstable or just about to become so. All wines with a smell are volatile to a certain extent, otherwise they wouldn't produce a vapour for us to smell. But very old, and sometimes very full-bodied, reds can smell as though they're hurling so many messages at you there can't be anything left in the glass.

It should be stated clearly after all this alarmism, however, that 90 per cent of all the wines I've ever tasted

merely of bad luck. Though if a particular bottler seems responsible for a string of corked bottles, that suggests he's trying to cut corners on his corks.

Wine boxes, especially those containing red wines, seem to hasten the oxidation process. Most wines start to oxidize if kept in an opened wine box for more than about a month (though, as I write, the manufacturers are trying to improve this).

To familiarize yourself with the two sulphur-inspired stinks, try to memorize the two very different smells of half a boiled egg left out for a day or two (H_2S) and that of a newly spent match (SO_2).

Don't go around with wine faults up your nose. It would be a great shame to spoil your drinking pleasure by

have been 'clean', and most of the rest showed only a hint of one of these possible faults – though there are some shocking basic table wines around.

anticipating any of the off-smells detailed above. If a wine has one, it will impress itself on you soon enough.

Balance

A wine is well balanced if all its components blend into the whole with none standing out of it. A wine could be out of balance because it has too much acidity, because it is too sweet, because the tannin is too evident or because the alcohol dominates the flavour. There is no single sensation that can help you make up your mind about whether or not the wine is balanced; you simply have to weigh up all the individual components. All good wines should be balanced by the time they are ready to drink, but a wine that seems to have a great future ahead of it may well be unbalanced in its youth.

Note whether the wines you drink in future are well balanced. 'Harmonious' is another word used to describe wines whose components make up a pleasurable whole. Balance has nothing to do with price or status. Even very modest wines can be perfectly balanced, and many venerable greats which have had years for one component to fall out of line can be slightly out of balance.

Length

Another sure sign of wine quality is what tasters call the *length* or *finish* of a wine. If, having swallowed (or even spat out) a wine, you're still aware of its flavour lingering in your mouth and nose – in a good way, of course – then the wine must have been well made. A mouthful of great wine can seem to hang about for minutes, if not hours, after the liquid has gone. This is why, in terms of total amount of pleasure given, 'expensive' wines are not always poor value compared with lesser liquids whose impact is lost once they're swallowed.

Take time to monitor how you feel just after swallowing a wine. You could find that you can double the pleasure a wine gives you by positively enjoying its 'long finish'. Wines which 'finish short' won't give you this added extra, and you might find yourself gulping them instead of savouring them.

The eyes don't have it

Standard texts on wine tasting point out at an early stage that three organs are involved: eye, nose and mouth, in that order. So usually they start with a detailed exposition of what the sense of sight can reveal about a wine. Literally looking at a wine is indeed the first thing a professional taster does, and it can often give him vital clues if he's tasting blind. But this book is about tasting for enjoyment and, beautiful though the rich red of a well-made Claret and mellow yellow of a mature white Burgundy may be, the pleasure that our eyes can give is as nought compared with what the nose and mouth can do for the voracious amateur. For that reason, this section on 'winesight' is relegated to third position *after* wine in the mouth and up the nose.

The only vital role played by the eye of someone who's tasting for pleasure is an obvious one: anticipating a fault. If a wine is hazy, it is usually suffering from some sort of malady and won't taste very good. If a wine, red or white, is much browner than you'd expect it to be, then it is probably oxidized. If it's full bodied and slightly sparkling, then it could be going through unintentional second fermentation in the bottle. This will make it taste worse than it should (though the slight 'prickle' in many lighter whites and reds is designed to refresh).

Among wines that are meant to be slightly sparkling are the following.

★ *Whites: anything described on the label as 'petillant' or 'perlant' (with little pearl-like bubbles), otherwise not many from France other than some from Savoie and those from new-wave outfits, such as Listel and SICAREX, making experimental wines in the deep south; many everyday wines from the German-speaking wine-producing countries; Vinho Verde; some adventurous dry Italian whites designed for early consumption; many youthful little numbers from Australia, New Zealand, South Africa and California – especially Rhine Riesling, Chenin Blanc and anything else with a bit of residual sugar.*

★ *Reds: much less common, but Lambrusco, red Vinho Verde (rarely exported) and some youthful Chiantis are allowed a little 'prickle'.*

Most particles found in wine are quite harmless, merely a nuisance if not picked out (if they're lighter than wine) or allowed to settle at the bottom of the bottle before it's poured (if they're heavier). Tiny bits of cork or deposit from the lip of the bottle that fall into your glass signify nothing more sinister than that the bottle was opened and served rather carelessly. White crystals in white wine and bits of dark deposit lurking in reds are as innocuous. Although they look so different, they're actually very similar, harmless solids precipitated by the maturation or storage of the wine, usually little crystals of tartaric acid. The tartrates are dyed dark red by the pigments in red wine, but in white wines they are left shining white and looking suspiciously like sugar to the wary wine-buying public. Because the wine trade is heartily sick of having bottles returned in this innocent condition, nowadays they usually do their best to avoid it by freezing out the tartrates in advance, or they remove them by fastidious filtering. However, I always rather warm to a wine that's butch enough to throw a deposit.

If you want to convince yourself about the harmlessness of these crystals, try chewing them next time you encounter any in a white wine. You'll find that they taste very acid – for that, in fact, is what they are – and not at all sugar-like. Note the similarity of the taste to that of your trusty carton of cream of tartar. Red-dyed crystals taste much the same, but seem even crunchier.

Now for the Sherlock Holmes part of the course. Those interested in becoming a whizz at blind tasting read on, for the sense of sight will be as useful to you with your wine

Look at wine against as white and plain a background as possible

glass as it was for the great detective with his magnifying glass.

A first glance

If the colour's rather dull and homogeneous – doesn't seem to vary much between the centre of the glass and the rim – then it's probably a very ordinary specimen. Most good wines actually *look* interesting, with nuances of colour shading towards a lighter rim. This is especially true in mature reds. The older a wine is, the greater will be the difference between the colour at the centre and an almost watery rim. If the wine has a very slight sparkle, then it could be any of the wines listed on the previous page.

To get the best look at a wine's colour, tilt the glass at an angle of 45° away from you, against as light and plain a background as possible. A white tablecloth would be perfect, or even a white plate. In this respect, the average dinner table or sitting room is not often well geared up for optimal tasting conditions. You won't get much of an idea about delicate nuances of shading by candlelight, or against a wooden table – but then you probably won't want to try blind tasting in such circumstances. Bear in mind that if you're going to make a serious attempt at guessing what a wine is, you (or the person who's trying to test your skill) should give serious thought to lighting. There is more about this on page 48.

Second sighting

In terms of hue, 'red' wines tend to go from purple to crimson to brick with age, while 'whites' can start off colourless but usually go yellower and then browner as they age. Particular colours are associated with particular areas or grape varieties, as detailed below.

- ★ Purple: most youthful wines of quality, and many light reds such as Beaujolais, Chinon, Bourgueil, Valpolicella, Bardolino and some New Zealand reds.
- ★ Mulberry: if the colour is deep too (see below) then the wine may well be made from the Nebbiolo or Syrah grape, or it could be a hot-climate Cabernet Sauvignon.
- ★ Mid-red: not many helpful clues from this.

The best clue to a wine's real hue is often to be found just inside the watery rim. This is particularly true in very deep-coloured red wines which may be almost black except just here at the inner edge. With red wines, colour is a prime indicator of their state of maturity. Anything with a blueish tinge must be fairly youthful; the merest hint of yellow or orange suggests age.

★ Reddish brown: the wine will probably be mature. An orange tinge is characteristic of Brunello di Montalcino. A blackish tinge suggests the wine might be from South Africa or Australia and, though mature, may not be old.

Colour is rather less revealing about the identity or maturity of white wines. Most whites fall into that narrow band between watery pale and pale straw, and their colour changes much less dramatically with age.

★ Almost colourless: Soave, Muscadet, young German wines. Mosel wines can have a greenish tinge, as can Chablis.
★ Pale, pale yellow: standard colour for most young dry whites.
★ Yellow gold: in Europe, the extra colour indicates sunshine or age, or some residual sugar, in a dry wine. Even very youthful Chardonnays made in California and Australia tend to have this colour, and the grapes Semillon and Viognier usually produce deep-hued wines wherever they are grown.
★ Deep gold: great sweet wines can even go brown with age without deteriorating in any way.

★ Pale purple: could be a Cabernet d'Anjou or a wine from Germany or Alsace that hardly knows whether it's a red or a rosé.
★ Pale orange: many Provence and other southern French rosés are this colour, but blind tasting pink wine is almost a contradiction in terms. If ever a wine was made not to be taken seriously, it is rosé.

A third peer

Not only hue, but intensity of hue is an important clue. Red wines get

The best way to get an accurate measure of the depth of a wine's

paler with age (except for some wines from the amazing Domaine de la Romanée Conti which take on a mysterious blush in their teens). A very deep colour in a red suggests that it is either very young, made from thick-skinned grapes and therefore from close to the Equator or from an exceptionally sunny vintage further away, made so as to extract maximum colour from the skins, or made from a grape variety such as the Nebbiolo, Syrah or Cabernet Sauvignon in a ripe year. A red might be pale because it is old, made far from the Equator or in a vintage which suffered from excessive rain just before harvest.

Conversely, depth of colour in a white wine indicates age. It may also suggest that the wine is relatively sweet, or has spent some time in oak.

colour is to put a glass of it on a white surface and look down into it from directly above. With samples of the same depth, you will notice a surprisingly wide variation in intensity between a wine (white or, more commonly, red) made around Mediterranean shores, such as those from Greece, Lebanon or North Africa, and one from the more temperate vineyards of northern France. Most red Burgundy is surprisingly pale.

A fourth twirl

The final trick is simple, in fact rather a dashing thing to perform and sound off about at the dinner table. By swirling the wine around in your glass and watching the sides of the glass afterwards, you will notice a wide variation in how viscous, or *sticky*, each wine is. Very viscous wines leave streams of something that looks like gin or clear nail-varnish falling slowly down the inside of the glass. Viscosity is a good indicator of body or weight, and therefore of a high alcohol content, lots of extract or both. Light-bodied wines won't leave much trace on the sides of the glass, whereas full-bodied wines leave very pronounced streams, sometimes

This swirling business is much easier to do with a glass that has a stem (one of the reasons why stemmed glasses are favoured for wine tasting). With your preferred hand, clasp the glass by the stem using your thumb and as many fingers as you like, and gently orbit the glass around a vertical axis so that wine splashes up the sides. Now put the glass down and look at the insides of the glass. Are there great sticky streamers or just slight patches of dampness?

called *tears* or even *legs* (though this last term was surely thought up to ballast all that 'wine is like a woo-man' analogizing).

The tasting technique – a summary

First, look the wine squarely in the glass. If you're tasting for enjoyment, you can merely look to make sure the wine is *clear* and not *pétillant* if it's not meant to be. You can also take careful note of its colour or hue by tilting it away from you at an angle of 45° against a white background, and examine *depth* or intensity of this hue by looking at the glass from directly above, as previously outlined. If you're trying to identify the wine, or get some measure of its quality, then these last two exercises are invaluable. Although authorities could talk for hours about the different hues and shadings they associate with different wines, in practice this 'seeing' stage usually takes only a few seconds.

Now to the all-important smelling or 'nosing'. You could simply lift the glass to your nostrils and sniff, but a much stronger vapour is given off if you swirl the wine around a bit, as described for testing viscosity, just before sniffing. The volatile elements that make up the vapour are given off at the surface of the wine, so by swirling you maximize the amount of wine in contact with air, and thus the vapour or 'smell' that is given off. You could simply jiggle the glass from side to side, but you'd be in more danger of spilling some of this highly taxed liquid than

Swirling

if you move it around rhythmically. It doesn't matter, by the way, whether you keep the glass in contact with the table while you swirl or do it in mid-air – though airborne swirling means you can get the glass to your nose even faster.

Now get the nostrils hovering over the surface of the wine, preferably with the glass tilted at 45° towards you to maximize the wine's surface area and therefore its impact – even now that it's subsided. If the nose hovers just over the top of the glass, it will be able to benefit from all the vapour that collects inside it. Practice will probably show you that the best way to nose is to concentrate for a moment on nothing but the wine and then to take one short sniff. Shutting your eyes at this point helps enormously to get the most out of the wine, but it does make you look a bit of a ninny.

When nosing you should first do an almost subconscious check that the wine is *clean*. The message 'I am obnoxious' will get to the brain fast enough, so you hardly need expend thought on this before going on to the whole point of smelling the wine: to experience its *flavour*. As we have seen, the olfactory centre, our personal flavour-detecting agency, is located at the top of the nostrils. Luckily for blind tasters, and for those of us who like making comparisons between different wines, its signals appear to arrive in the brain close to that bit we call memory – which is why smells can be so uncannily evocative, and why wine tasting can be so much fun. Try to develop the ability to identify smells or flavours, to assess them

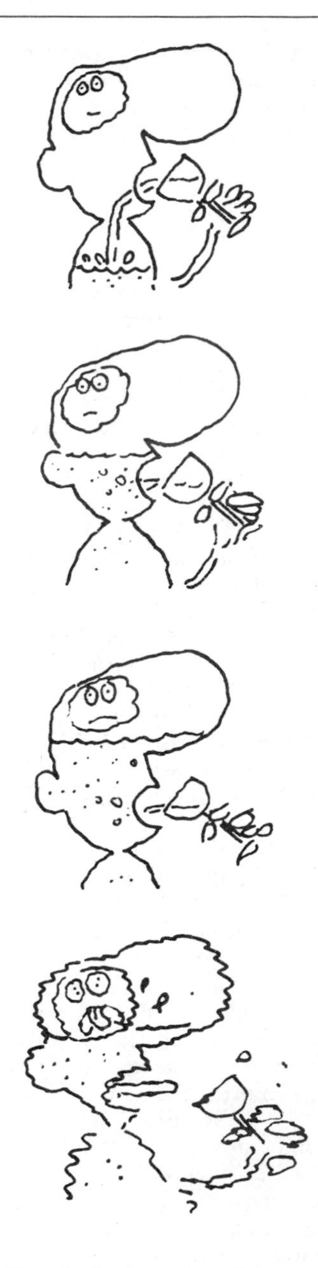

How the brain receives the message

qualitatively and to programme them into your memory so that you can relate them to other smells in the future. Don't worry if at this point you feel confused about actually describing them. There are guidelines for individual wines throughout the second half of this course.

Now at last you're allowed to get some of the wine into your mouth. It will make a composite impression on you of *sweetness, acidity, tannin level* and *body* via the tongue and insides of the mouth, and will confirm the *flavour* by way of the vapour that gets up the retro-nasal passage. To make sure all the bits of your mouth most sensitive to each of the four taste components are well exposed to the wine, you will need to take a fairly generous mouthful. For the same reason, hold the wine in your mouth for a little while before either swallowing it or spitting it out. (See page 68 for details of when this apparent sacrilege is recommended.) If, when you have some wine in your mouth, you open your lips slightly and take in some air at the same time, you will further encourage the wine's volatile elements to vaporize and pass up the pass up the retro-nasal passage to the olfactory centre thereby maximizing the impact any wine can make on you at any one time. This is why some enthusiastic inhabitants of the professional tasting room make such unsavoury gargling noises. This practice should be avoided in the dining room.*

Enthusiast wine tasters make all sorts of unsavoury gargling noises

* I've just realized to my horror that, so eager am I to experience everything a wine has to offer, I invariably – and hitherto unconsciously – take in a bit of air with every single mouthful of wine, whether in a professional tasting room, at a smart dinner table or over a bowl of pasta with the family. I hope you can behave less embarrassingly.

While the wine was in your mouth, you should have had a chance to weigh up each of the taste components and work out your assessment of its *balance*; and, as you consider how your mouth feels after you've swallowed or expectorated, you should notice its *length* of flavour.

All of that took some time to explain, but it takes only a second to do. Just that simple technique will ensure that the relevant receivers are tuned in for every message a wine has to transmit. By nosing the wine first, you can experience all the pleasure of its flavour unencumbered by the distractions of the liquid in the mouth. By the time you have a mouthful of it, you are well equipped to understand the coarser but important messages transmitted there.

However, it is important to realize that tasting is extremely subjective – not only psychologically, in that we all like different wines and would choose different words to describe their flavours, but also physiologically in that our sensitivities to different aspects vary enormously from person to person. Some people can find it very difficult to assess sweetness, for instance, whereas I happen to find it a struggle detecting even hideously high SO_2 levels. There are all sorts of weird explanations for this. Physiologists have worked out that the reason some people take lots of sugar in their tea and coffee is that the tips of their tongues don't actually come into contact with the liquid. By being 'taught to drink properly' they can dramatically lower their sugar intake. My explanation for my own sulphur insensitivity is being brought up in a house equipped with a coke-fired Aga. Don't laugh; it could well be right.

Try blending red and white wines together

2 Practical matters

You now know how to taste wine, a more rewarding yet hardly more taxing business than merely drinking it, and can use every tasting opportunity as part of this course. The circumstances in which you taste may vary from the most clinical lab conditions (the sort of Daz-white atmosphere in which professional quality-control tasters work), through the various rooms of your house, to picnics. This chapter describes the ideal conditions for tasting, including the right equipment and practices as well as the right surroundings. Of course you won't always be able to taste under ideal conditions. Indeed, you will make yourself extremely unpopular with your friends and family if you insist on complete silence at the dinner table as the wines are tasted, or on the perfect wine glass at a picnic (though that's not so unreasonable – my ideal wine glass costs about 45p and is quite sturdy enough for the picnic basket). Adaptation and compromise are the keys here. Your wine-tasting experience will not be completely ruined if conditions are less than ideal, even though specialists can be dogmatic about this. If necessary, go ahead and make simple changes to your pre-wine-tasting lifestyle, but it would run counter to the philosophy of this book if your pursuit of the grape and its delights made anyone else feel uncomfortable.

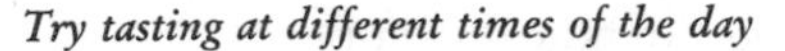

Try tasting at different times of the day

Timing

Our senses are keenest early in the day, perhaps not from the moment we first raise an eyelid but certainly towards the middle of the morning. This is why most professional wine tastings are timed for about eleven thirty a.m. However, there are few of us whose lives can easily encompass something as relaxing as a wine tasting in the first half of the day. In practice, you will probably do most of your wine drinking during, and just before, meals and will be at your most enthusiastic about wine in the evening. If you are thinking of trying some serious wine tasting, either by yourself or with friends but without the distraction of a meal, then try a Sunday-morning tasting. During the rest of the week, when daytime tasting is difficult, early evening is better than late. Wine, as doctors well know, stimulates the appetite. (Such a shame the NHS no longer allows prescriptions for wine.) Wine tasting therefore makes a good prelude to eating; if you leave it till after you've eaten a heavy meal your senses will have lost the keen edge so useful to the wine taster.

Next time you have a day to yourself – at the weekend perhaps or, even better, when you're on holiday – try tasting a single wine at different times of the day. Write down your impressions on each occasion (there's more on tasting-notes on page 63) without looking at what you've written previously and see if you can tell when you were at your most perceptive (actually perceptive as opposed to apparently so). You'll probably be in peak condition towards the end of the morning, just as you start feeling ready for lunch. I certainly know from experience that the first wine of the day usually tastes the best, but that rule did not hold good for the jug of rich red I was once served with breakfast on a Spanish wine estate. You do need to be fully awake before you appreciate that first glass. Conversely, I am guiltily aware of the amount of good wine I have drunk at the end of the day without fully appreciating every nuance of its flavour.

Physical environment

If you want to get a good look at a wine's clarity, colour and intensity, then you'll need a surprisingly strong light and a plain white surface against which to hold the glass. Strong daylight is best, but usually impracticable. And even if you *are* able to taste during the day, sadly

Just you try tasting anything really fine out of doors on a hot day. Another confession is the Cheval Blanc 1947 that a bunch of us, who should have known better, tried to savour under the hot open Suffolk sky.

you may be better off staying indoors. The great outdoors has a habit of wafting the bouquet of a great wine into the far distance, and direct sunlight overheats both wine and tasters.

When setting up a tasting indoors, try to choose somewhere with plenty of soft light (not colour-distorting strip lights) and work out how you are going to find that white surface. Ideally sit at, or even better, move round a table covered with a white tablecloth. Irish linen would be lovely, of course, but a strip taken from a roll of disposable paper table-covering won't make you taste any less acutely. Remember, too, that most tabletops need to be protected from the ravages of spilt wine by laying several layers of newspaper underneath the tablecloth. If you want to taste in a comfortable, informal way in your favourite armchair – treating a couple of samples of wine as a substitute, say, for the evening paper – then there's an easy solution to the white surface problem. If you have your wine glasses on a side table next to you, you can simply hold them up against a piece of white card in your lap. An envelope will do, though if you're really getting into the swing of this thing you'll probably want to write tasting notes and you can use the piece of card to write on.

Different tasters feel differently about whether they taste better when seated or standing. I don't find it makes much difference myself; my nose and mouth seem blissfully unaware of what's happening to my legs. But certainly, it's usually more comfortable to spit when standing than sitting – if only to put the contents of the spittoon at a greater distance from your nose and eyes.

Tasting in the comfort of your favourite armchair

Surprisingly few dining rooms make very good tasting chambers. Candlelight is seen by advertising executives as inextricably intertwined with wine drinking. This is presumably because the candle is a conveniently portable light against which wines with a strong sediment

Look critically at the lighting over your table. Is there a way you could make it easier to get a good look at your wines without totally disrupting things – perhaps by moving a standard lamp?

used to be decanted, and because wine is traditionally associated with romance. But you need to have a lot of candles set pretty high above the table's surface to throw enough light for easy tasting. You can make the most of the light they give by using a white tablecloth, but you may well want to show off that beautifully polished table to your dinner guests. In these circumstances, a plain light plate should provide a suitable backdrop for wine examination. If all else fails, you can always hold a glass up to the nearest available light source for examination (this is the origin of that rather pretentious-looking stance). However, this doesn't give you nearly such an accurate and detailed picture.

Next time you buy place mats, plates and table linen, spare just a thought for how useful a plain white surface would be when enjoying wine.

Another good place for tasting at home is the kitchen. You may well have a useful white work-surface that can easily be wiped clean of all wine's purple circles and blobs, and may even be conveniently close to the kitchen sink (a good spittoon if you can bear it). The only problem here may be very distracting smells. Because our noses are so important in wine tasting, it makes sense to distract them from the glass in hand as little as possible. If you're seriously trying to distinguish the difference between two glasses in front of you, it's made all the more difficult by a strong whiff of cooking or cleaning smells.

Scour your house for good places for tasting. You need good light and no strong smells. If you're tasting a lot of wines at one time, a big flat surface, on which to line up the bottles and glasses, is useful.

This is why participants at formal tastings are adjured to 'come clean', untainted by scent or aftershave; why the organizers try to serve food only in another room; why there are no floral decorations, and why they even hang ostentatious no-smoking

Tasting – possible distraction

signs above the tasting table. You should hear the shocked whisper that goes up if a whiff of Dior or Dunhill is detected.

Mine may be a rather heretical view, but I think the need for an olfactory vacuum in which to taste has been a little overstated. We all have our own body smell; it can be so pronounced that others call it body odour, or discernible only by very close friends indeed. We don't really notice our own body's smell – not knowing what life would be like without it, after all. We get used to our own little 'aura'. This is true even of heavy smokers who reek of stale tobacco. Those same people, I have noticed, are as able as the next person to distinguish nuances of flavour in wines, because they're used to tasting through their own tobacco-scented atmosphere. If, on the other hand, the heavy smoker says, 'Here, taste this!' and hands you a wine glass he's been nursing for ten minutes, you'll first smell him and only later, through the haze of his aura, the wine he's so excited about.

Similarly, a glass held by someone who purposely forswore the scent bottle before a tasting, but who always uses a fairly distinctively perfumed soap, to someone else will smell primarily of that soap and only then of the wine inside it. No matter what precautions are taken to make a tasting room as 'unsmelly' as possible, there will be as many different little personal auras as there are people. Eventually the room will take on a smell, discernible to those with a particularly keen nose, that is the mixture of all these together with

Next time you're drinking wine with friends, swap glasses and notice how some people leave a hint of their own personal aura on a glass.

If you're a smoker, try not to smoke while someone else is concentrating hard on a wine, but don't despair in the fear that you'll never be able to taste as well as the non-smoker. If you're a long-term smoker, try the blindfold test on page 13 at the same time as a non-smoker friend. You will probably do every bit as well.

Leave a hint of their own personal aura on the glass

Next time you're drinking wine, or otherwise using your nose, in an atmosphere where there's a particularly strong smell, notice how the smell that at first is so noticeable seems to fade with time. I've tasted wine in all sorts of circumstances – from the standard French tasting room, where the host almost invariably lights up a Gauloise as you start to taste, to a room that was in the middle of being painted. At first I thought the wines would have no chance against the opposition for my nasal attention, but very soon I'd the smell of all the wines that have been opened. There's no need, therefore, to get worried about the odd whiff of recently smoked cigarette or newly applied scent. It will soon dissipate and add itself as just one component to the overall atmosphere – and our sense of smell is anyway constantly adjusting itself to its environment. If we hold the heavy smoker's or the clean-handed person's glass for long enough, we'll start compensating for their respective auras and start smelling the wine.

forgotten the distraction as my nose got used to the overall atmosphere. After all, people who live in towns where industry produces particularly noxious fumes don't even notice them.

To ban the smell of food may be sensible when tasting clinically as part of a job or test, but food plays such an important part in the enjoyment of wine, it's unnecessary to bar it from every wine tasting. After all, at the dining table a wine's bouquet has to battle against the smell of the dish with which it is served, and this can be a much bigger problem than the odd plate of edible blotting paper that can be so appreciated by amateur wine tasters. Under such circumstances, you may find dry savoury biscuits helpful tasting companions.

When enjoying wine and food at the same time, especially hot or very aromatic food the flavour of which drifts up into the atmosphere, try to work out your own practical way of getting the most from your glass of wine. You may want to turn slightly to one side, away from the food, when 'nosing' the glass. Try to get the chance to examine a wine before food gets to the table; it will show itself best without edible distraction.

So, a few ground rules when tasting wine.

★ To appreciate colour, you'll need some sort of white surface.
★ At a formal tasting you will be unpopular if you smoke or are obviously anointed with something smelly.
★ In any surroundings you will find it easier to taste without the distraction of other smells, though you may well decide you'd rather sacrifice the fleeting aroma of the Viognier grape for

It can be extremely tedious if you refuse to give any clues or encouragement

the exotic allure of your scent or the enveloping comfort of your favourite tobacco.

Possible distractions – feeling right

Before hoisting the no-smoking signs to limit other people's behaviour, make sure you are doing everything right for wine tasting. Far more important than what's going on ten yards from you is what's going on inside your mouth. Before setting off to enjoy a glass of wine, think about what you last ate and drank. Most toothpastes make anything high in acidity tasted after them seem pretty awful. It would certainly be a crime to taste a fine wine less than an hour after brushing your teeth with paste. Strong cough and throat preparations can leave their mark in the mouth so forcefully that wine tasting is difficult, as do strong mints and chewing gum. Also, eating or drinking anything that is particularly high in one of the basic taste components most commonly encountered in wine – sweetness, acidity or tannin – seems to make assessing wine soon afterwards difficult. Chocolate, sharply dressed salads and even an apparently innocuous cup of tea seem to leave the mouth too highly tuned into their own particular strength.

Try, once only, the following tastes immediately before taking a mouthful of wine:

toothpaste (it makes fruit juice taste dreadful, too)
cough linctus, drops, pastilles
throat lozenges such as Victory V and Fisherman's Friends
Trebor extra-strong mints
Doublemint chewing gum
Mars Bars
vinegar
tea

They each leave the mouth feeling different, usually hyped up to receive one particular message and therefore not very good at making a sound critical assessment of a wine, let alone getting the full pleasure potential from it.

The simplest way to 'neutralize' your mouth after one of these problem tastes is to chew a mouthful of something absorbent but fairly bland, such as bread, or to try to rinse out the flavour with water (though I've found this less effective). I was once part of a tasting

Work out your own 'neutralizing' technique so that you don't have to spend the rest of your life avoiding certain foods or preparations just in case someone might offer you a glass of wine.

group that met at eight o'clock in the morning (it seemed the obvious solution for people who were working all day and studying at night – at least I *think* that was the reason). The disadvantage of toothpaste soon became apparent and so I took to brushing my teeth without toothpaste and experimented with various mouthwashes. For your information, I found Listerine (though not Listermint) does the freshening trick and doesn't interfere with the wines.

Taste – after toothpaste

As well as having the inside of your mouth in order, it helps if the inside of your head is also geared up for wine tasting. It's amazing how one's ability to taste can be affected by mood. As outlined above, I think it helps to be just slightly peckish to have that edge on your appreciation and you also need to be alert and relaxed enough to concentrate, almost in your own little world, on the wine in hand.

If you reckon your palate and judgement are unswayable by tiresome details such as the weather or the telephone bill, then try a few simple exercises.

★ *If it's deep midwinter, think of a wine you remember particularly enjoying in the summer – a beautifully refreshing Mosel or Frascati, perhaps, something that brings back memories of sipping in the sunshine. Try tasting it one frosty day. Doesn't it seem a bit thin, a little lacking in flesh?*

★ *If, on the other hand, you're currently enjoying a heatwave, try a rich red that gave you pleasure last winter. That Rioja or Dão that seemed such good value then surely seems a bit rough and overblown in warm weather.*

No matter what the main purpose of your tasting – identification, assessment or straightforward enjoyment – you'll find the most serious distraction from forming your opinion will be other people. The whole business of wine tasting is so subjective, and even the most experienced tasters can feel so suggestible, that an early comment (delivered with sufficient confidence, of course) can sway a whole roomful of tasters. With any wine, your first impression – what you sense with the first concentrated sniff – is by far the most important. Allow yourself a moment's intense concentration as you nose a wine for the first time

Practise giving each wine that you drink just thirty seconds' attention as you approach it for the first time;

and take note of your reaction. If you think it's a Claret and someone says, 'Positively *yells* Burgundy, wouldn't you say?', don't allow yourself to be talked into smelling Burgundy on the second sniff. However knowledgeable other tasters may be, there is no reason why their judgements will be more accurate than yours. In my experience, it is the relative novices who get things right in blind tasting. The old hands have far too many contradictory signals to confuse them.

that's thirty seconds during which your ears are metaphorically plugged, safe from the distraction of general conversation and, even worse, other people's comments on the wine.

Try chilling wine to different temperatures

The right temperature

The convention is that white wines and rosés are served cool, and red wines at a higher temperature somewhat loosely called 'room'. It's useful to realize that this is very little more than a convention, and that by not sticking to it too rigidly you may be able to increase your enjoyment.

Notice the temperature in the room in which you usually drink wine. Unless you are a healthy relic of a bygone age, it is likely to be more than 65°F when you're actually drinking wine, too hot a temperature to match your wine. Kitchens, in particular, encourage mulling.

Generally speaking, the warmer a wine (or anything) the more volatiles it gives off and the more flavour it seems to have. There is an upper limit to this, however, as demonstrated by those restaurateurs who think that if a little warming is a good thing then lots of it will be very good. A red wine that's served too hot, say at 70°F, will start the irreversible process of turning acetic and breaking down. If you want to get maximum *flavour* from any wine – red, white or pink – you should drink it at a temperature between 60° and 65°F.

Take any red and any white wine, as basic as you like. Pour out two half-glasses of each and cover all four of them with cling-film to keep the bouquet in the glass. Put one red and one white into the fridge for half an hour and leave the other two in a normally heated living room. Now compare the two pairs, whites first and then red. When you take off the cling-film, you'll see how much more bouquet the warmer wines seem to have.

Another factor comes into play here:

Next time you are drinking a chilled

we cherish wine's ability to refresh us, as well as intrigue us with its flavour. Just as we like soft drinks to be chilled, we have come to expect aperitif wines drunk to refresh (which are usually white or rosé) to be chilled too. And that custom has somehow been extended to encompass the chilling of all whites that we drink – even if it's a full-bodied white Burgundy to accompany a hot fish dish.

What determines whether or not a wine's flavour can survive chilling well is, in fact, dependent not on colour but on body. The more full bodied a wine is, the warmer it will need to be before its esters and aldehydes vaporize to yield its flavour. The lighter it is, the more easily volatiles are given off even at lowish temperatures. Because white wines tend to be lighter than reds, the conventional wisdom of chilling them usually works – but there are exceptions. Full-bodied whites, such as great Burgundy, white Rhône, Chardonnays in general and many massive whites from warm climates, will be spoiled by chilling them too assiduously. Conversely, light-bodied reds, such as Beaujolais, red Loire wines, many early-maturing red Burgundies and north Italian reds, can be very attractive and refreshing if slightly chilled.

The convention may also have something to do with the fact that heat tends to decrease our sensitivity to tannin and to sweetness (and sulphur). That's why tannic red

wine with food, try to work out what benefits you're getting from the coolness of the wine. Once the mixture of wine and food is in your mouth, it tends to warm up speedily towards body temperature (from 45° to 75°F in ten seconds). Do you savour the wine for its refreshing coolness, or are you simply chilling it out of habit? Remember the exercise, described on page 14, of trying to distinguish between a red and a white wine when blindfold. If you found it difficult to tell them apart, why treat them differently when deciding on serving temperatures?

Experiment by serving different wines at different temperatures to find out what suits you and the wines best. Of course, when you're drinking for refreshment you'll want the wine to be a bit cooler than when you're trying to eke the last ounce of flavour from it. Start gently edging up the temperature at which you serve full-bodied white wines. If they're good, you'll find them much more rewarding. If they're not so good, this will be demonstrated very obviously and you may decide not to choose that particular wine in future.

At the bottom end of the price range, it's much easier to find acceptable light reds (such as the army of 'vins de pays' from Southern France) than it is to find clean, dry whites. Try serving one of these light reds slightly chilled, just like smart restaurants serve Beaujolais, and see how you can turn it into an inexpensive refreshing red aperitif.

wines taste so tough if cool and why very sweet wines taste less so if very cool. Baron Philippe de Rothschild has the curious habit of serving his customary Château d'Yquem so cold with dessert that it has ice clinks in it. That deprives him of its wonderful bouquet, just as overzealous wine waiters who try to keep their white wines permanently under 40°F cheat their customers of much that the wine has to give.

If you have a really nasty white wine, the best way to serve it is very chilled, as this will mask its nastiness. If you want to experience as much as possible of what a wine has to give, good and bad, then it is best to taste it at that convenient midway temperature known as 'cellar', i.e. about 50° to 55°F. Reds can take rather higher temperatures than this, but the glass can always be warmed up quickly in the cup of your hand. Once served, the natural progression of the temperature of a wine is, after all, upwards, by about 1°F every three minutes. Once it's poured, it will be exposed to the hot air that inevitably surrounds all of us wine tasters, so don't worry if you fear you have served a wine too cool. Just realize how important it is to wait until it has warmed up enough to give its true flavour.

It is also worth pointing out that, once wine gets into the mouth, it inevitably warms up there. Experiments have shown that even heavily chilled wine rapidly thaws in the mouth, but by then it will be too late to get the full benefits of experiencing the bouquet in isolation.

You will want to evolve your own regimen on serving temperatures, but these are some useful guidelines.

- ★ *Keep wine in an unheated room, or outhouse, where the temperature doesn't vary too much during the day, or even from season to season. Ideal 'cellar' temperature is about 50°F, though experiments involving keeping wines for long periods at much higher temperatures suggest it is the constancy of temperature that is more important.*
- ★ *For tasting purposes, most wines are fine served straight from a 50°F cellar. Whites should reveal all, and reds can be swiftly warmed by being poured and cradled in the glass.*

You may want to cool some wines, Champagne and other sparkling wines for instance, well below 50°F if you want to enjoy their refreshing aspect more than their flavour. You can put the bottle in the fridge for an hour or so, depending on how cool your fridge is. If this is an unplanned refresher you can chill the bottle by putting it into the ice box, or even the deep freeze, for about twenty minutes. This is supposed to give the wine too great a shock, but I have never known it to cause any more harm to the flavour than the standard method of immersing the bottle in a mixture of water and ice cubes in an ice bucket or other roomy container. The icy water works much better than ice cubes alone, by the way, because there's something cool in contact with every bit of the bottle's surface. If aesthetics are not a factor, ice cooling packs, kept in the ice box, can be used instead of ice cubes.

The decanter – dead as a dodo?

There is still surprisingly little debate about serving temperatures for wine; most drinkers continue to follow the accepted wisdom unquestioningly. The Great Decanting Debate, however, goes on strongly and those following this wine course could well add useful observations to it.

The decanting tradition grew up from a time when wine was drawn off into a jug from a cask in the cellar, and later when winemakers left a deposit in the bottle. It then made sense to pour wine off this deposit into a decanter so that one could drink without chewing. Nowadays, it still makes sense to decant those few wines that have thrown a heavy deposit, provided they are robust enough to withstand it. Some very old wines and some very lightly perfumed wines would simply lose their bouquet if they had to suffer the fairly boisterous treatment of being poured twice. This is akin to the dangers, already described, of trying to serve a wine in the great outdoors. Wine and too much air do not make a good mixture.

The debate centres on the question of how good a mixture wine and *some* air is. For a long time it has been thought that the process of ageing in wine was simply one of slow oxidation,* that small amounts of air either already present in the sealed bottle or entering through the cork gradually react with the wine to make it develop into something more complex and ramified. It was thought therefore that if you poured

Climate is only one of the things that affect the taste of wine

* In fact it is now reckoned that reduction, not oxidation, is the key to wine maturation. The mixture of elements in a young wine, present as a result either of the grapes or of the process of fermentation, binds together in various 'reduced' formations to produce a much more complex substance than the initial raw material.

a bottle of wine into another container such as a decanter, you would aerate it and somehow telescope the ageing process into a few minutes by putting the wine into contact with a lot of air. The bouquet would be fanned into life by all this oxygen.

This view is still widely held, but the results of comparative tastings of samples of the same wines opened at varying intervals before tasting have been suspiciously inconclusive. Furthermore, some authorities argue that the effects of aeration can only be harmful; that by exposing a delicate bouquet to air you may make it evanesce, and that the interesting reactions between oxygen and wine are too complicated to be speeded up. All that can happen, they argue, is that the wine starts to oxidize too fast, and therefore deteriorates.

Many ordinary wine drinkers claim that some wines, especially cheap reds, taste much better if opened and left to 'breathe' for a few hours. This may have nothing to do with decanting or even aeration. After all, such a small proportion of wine, the area of the bottleneck, is in contact with air that only a tiny amount of oxidation would take place. A much more likely explanation is that with cheap wines there may be off-odours trapped in the gap between the surface of the wine and the cork, and that this 'breathing' process allows them to evaporate.

It is true that the potential disadvantage of dissipating the bouquet of a wine by decanting it or allowing a half-full bottle to stand

A-level: Very much an optional exercise this, but one you can save for a rainy day when you feel like making a major contribution to what we know about wine and air. You'll need to open up a fair amount of wine, so it might make sense to try it out on a day when you will be entertaining in the evening.

Choose any wine(s) you like, as many as you can afford, but as few as one will do. It would make sense to select a wine you would consider decanting – perhaps a very cheap red and a more expensive youthful one. You'll need three bottles of each, I'm afraid. Open one three hours before you plan to do your tasting and decant it into a decanter or a clean, empty wine bottle. Open the second bottle one hour before serving and simply let it 'breathe'. Open the third just before you taste a glass from each bottle, served to you blind by a kind-hearted accomplice. See if you can notice any difference between the effect of the three different pre-serving treatments.

This experiment is open to endless variation: with different wines, different lengths of time before tasting, and different sorts of 'decanter' (something with a wide mouth, such as a glass jug, would expose the wine to more air than a narrow-necked vessel).

open can sometimes be an advantage. Some wines, full-bodied reds particularly, can be just too intensely flavoured when young. Rather than gaining extra flavours, the decanter allows them to lose some of their aggressive youth and mellow into a more palatable, if more vapid, middle age. This is especially true of some rich reds from California, Australia, Italy, the Lebanon, and the odd 'farmyard' wine from Spain and the Rhône.

Keep wine in an unheated room or outhouse

A good set of rules, then, is to open cheap and full-bodied reds a hour or so before serving, to decant when there's a sediment to remove or a beautiful decanter to enjoy aesthetically, and otherwise not to get too exercised about the whole business.

Wine leftovers

As those marketing the highly successful wine box are very well aware, we don't always consume wine in exact bottle-sized portions. If a wine is left in a half-empty bottle the air will accelerate its deterioration. The lighter the wine the faster it will deteriorate. (Though, as outlined earlier, some very aggressively full-bodied wines can benefit from a bit of aeration.)

This wine course involves a great deal of comparative tasting, as it is chiefly by comparing different wines that we can learn about them. This is likely to result in many wine leftovers, fractions of a bottle that you will want to keep for future drinking. Do not despair! Wine from a bottle that

Because the tap incorporates a one-way valve, wine boxes are designed to let wine out but no air in. When this self-deflating mechanism works perfectly, you can draw off as much or as little wine as you like without the problem of the wine inside being exposed to lots of harmful air. It is certainly true that an opened wine box guards wine for much longer than an opened wine bottle, but it is important to realize that

★ *by following the advice given opposite you can considerably prolong the active life of a wine sold in bottle; and*
★ *at the time of writing, the process of filling wine boxes is still being perfected and, at the moment,*

has been opened can last for weeks, provided it is kept in conditions as near airtight as possible. On the other hand, the more air it is left in contact with, the sooner it will spoil.

The answer then is to keep a stock of small bottles into which you can decant leftovers. Half-bottles are useful for this purpose, as are the quarter-bottles served on planes, and here the funny half-litre flasks into which the Hungarians put Tokay really come into their own. Fill them right up to the top and then stopper them firmly with narrow corks (Italian ones are useful because most Italian bottlenecks are unusually small) or stopper corks saved from old Sherry and Port bottles. Of course the decanting process itself will mean that the wine loses a little bit of its initial freshness, but the leftover wine should still be perfectly enjoyable if kept in this way.

wine kept inside an unopened wine box deteriorates after a very few months, much sooner than wine kept in an unopened bottle.

See too the exercise demonstrating the harmful effects of air on wine, outlined on page 35.

Keep a collection of small bottles to decant leftovers

Why you need glasses

Much more important than the exact temperature of the wine, and/or whether you've decanted it, is the sort of vessel you taste it from. Metal, and even pottery, goblets may look good on the shelf, but leave them there if you want to get the most from your wine. Glass is the ideal material because it is tasteless and doesn't impose any temperature on the liquid inside. You can easily warm up a glassful of wine by cupping your hand round it, if necessary, and you can savour the anticipatory pleasure of looking at a wine's colour.

Try drinking wine out of the following drinking vessels and note how 'wrong' it tastes. Is it partly because you can't get a look at the wine before tasting it?

china teacup
pottery mug
pewter tankard
silver goblet
plastic beaker
paper cup (this, curiously, is probably the best of these, affecting the wine's flavour least)

We have seen how important it is to swirl wine around in order to release its flavour, and this is where the stem comes in. A glass with a stem can easily be rotated, but without necessarily warming the wine up at the same time. You will want to 'collect' the flavour in the space above the wine's surface, which means that the best shape for a wine glass is one that goes in from the bowl towards the rim. If you make sure the glass is not filled more than half full, there should be no danger of precious wine spilling out as you swirl and there'll be lots of room for the vapour to collect above it. The best wine glasses therefore are tulip- or near-spherical-shaped and have a stem. Coloured glass is rather frowned upon as it disguises a wine's colour; similarly cut crystal, the pride of glass departments throughout the land, for much the same reason. The best wine glasses are never the most expensive. Many off-licences sell glasses called Paris goblets for less than 50p each. These can hold as much as 8 oz so that you can get a good noseful of vapour above a 2 oz, or even a 3 oz, sample. For tasting, it's important that glasses aren't too thimble-like, otherwise you won't be able to get the full impact 'on the nose', as professional tasters say.

Try swirling a sample of wine round in a glass without a stem. It will be much more awkward and liable to spill.

Muster as wide a selection of differently shaped glasses as you can, and pour a small, similarly sized sample of any single wine into each. Give each a short swirl taking a concentrated sniff from it immediately afterwards: swirl, sniff, swirl, sniff, etc. Notice how much lighter and more evasive the bouquet is on those samples in glasses whose shape encourage the volatiles to escape into the atmosphere, such as these –

– as opposed to being stronger when trapped in more enclosed glasses, such as these:

Remember that you don't need an enormous amount of wine in order to taste it, for it is the surface, rather than the depth, of the sample that releases the all-important flavour. An inch depth in an 8 oz glass would be ample. The standard number of glasses for *drinking* available per 75 cl bottle is between six and eight, but

There's an official tasting glass devised by the Institut National des Appellations d'Origine de ma Tante (INAO), but quality seems to be variable. Good sources of plain, well-

you could squeeze out up to twenty samples for tasting purposes.

You don't need a battery of different glasses for different wines. You could get by quite happily with a single sort, described above, though you should probably fill it only sparingly when serving fortified wines like Port and Sherry. The wine trade's single-mindedness over glasses does waver a little when it comes to sparkling wines and champagne. Approved glasses for bubbles are tall and thin, allowing only limited escape space for the carbon dioxide (not those saucers which encourage wines to lose their fizz fast), but the standard glass will be fine for *tasting* sparkling wines – possibly better for enjoying the flavour as opposed to the fizziness.

Thin, delicate glass is not necessary for tasting but it does add to the overall pleasure of drinking.

Do be careful when washing and storing glasses. You may well need to use detergent to get greasy fingermarks off, but be sure to rinse glasses well afterwards. The taste of Fairy Liquid does nothing for fine wine – and its traces play havoc with the mousse of a sparkling wine. Also make sure that you store them right way up, so that they don't trap a stale smell in the bowl, in a clean cupboard or box.

shaped glasses which are made from attractively thin glass are Baccarat (terribly expensive and horribly breakable) and the following merchants:

Berry Bros & Rudd, 3 St James's Street, London SW1
Ellis Son & Vidler, 57 Cambridge Street, London SW1, and Hastings
Green's, 34 Royal Exchange, London EC3
Harry Waugh Wine Selections, 4 Mardon, Westfield Park, Hatch End, Middlesex
The Wine Society, Gunnels Wood Lane, Stevenage, Hertfordshire

Compare bubble & mousse in glass that has thin coating of detergent

Just to prove the point, next time you have some sparkling wine open, compare the bubble and mousse in a thoroughly rinsed glass and one that still has a slight coating of detergent. The fizz will be a damp squib in the second glass.

Wine and words

In order to compare, discuss and remember wines we need some way of recording and communicating our reactions to them. A vocabulary consisting of the delighted yelp and disgusted moan just does not do the trick. I've seen some tasters use nothing but numbers (three for clarity, five for bouquet, seven for finish, etc.) but it's not very illuminating to have every wine described only by a sort of football formation. There are others who try to draw the impact of a wine's flavour on the palate.

Opposite is a wine that is very showy at first but then finishes short.

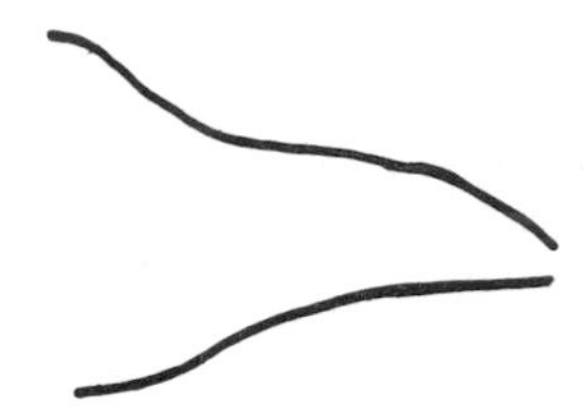

And here's one that's 'dumb' on the nose but opens up in the mouth.

Either or both of these 'languages' are fine to supplement but not supplant the most subtle method of communication that we have for flavour, style and so on: the written (and spoken) word.

See sample tasting notes on page 66.

The easiest way to learn about how wine tastes is to keep a record of your tasting experiences, to make tasting notes on as many of the wines you taste as you can. Knowing that you have to describe a wine helps enormously to concentrate your mind on it, and the notes provide a reference for you when building up the valuable experience of drawing comparisons. Quite how assiduously you keep the note-taking habit will depend on how much enthusiasm and thickness of skin you have. I don't make notes when friends ask me round for supper, but I know one or two professionals who do. They've never regretted it for a minute (their spouses may occasionally have, but not their publishers).

Get into the habit of writing down your impressions at the time of tasting

The difficulty of choosing words to describe wines has been outlined in Chapter 1, under 'Capturing the flavour'. There is an attempt at a brief glossary of tasting terms at the back of this book, though you will doubtless evolve your own terms for some sensations. The most useful of these will be your 'trigger' words for various commonly encountered grape varieties. Once these are established, you should be well on your way to successful blind tasting. For some time I had used 'blackcurrants' for the claret grape Cabernet Sauvignon and 'raspberries' for red Burgundy's Pinot Noir, but was still searching around for a word I could use to pin together all my impressions of the Hermitage grape Syrah. Then someone volunteered their 'burnt rubber', and it has worked ever since. This story is told to encourage you to persevere if you find matching words and flavours a difficult exercise. As you will have gathered, the expression can be as absurd as you like.

The most important item on your tasting notes is the full pedigree of the wine you are tasting. Make sure you eventually get down its name, vintage, shipper and any other information, even if you start out by tasting the wine blind. A set of random wine descriptions is of little use to anyone unless each wine is fully identified. If you are organizing a wine tasting for friends, you will help them enormously if you write out tasting sheets beforehand.

Make sure you leave plenty of room between each wine's name as full-blown tasting notes encompass

Get into the habit of writing down your impressions of the wines you taste as soon as possible after you try them, at the time of tasting ideally, or perhaps when you get back home.

Try to develop your own special trigger words for different grape varieties and then for other more complicated aspects of wines. Throughout the second half of the course, specific examples are suggested. When stuck for a trigger word, try reading through old tasting-notes to see if any expression keeps cropping up in association with a particular factor determining taste.

You will learn five times as much by comparing two wines

10th July 1983

Wine	*Eye*	*Nose*	*Mouth**	*Conclusions*
Pinot Grigio 1981 DOC Santa Margherita, Alto Adige	*Very pale. Watery with greenish tinge. Slight sparkle.*	*Pronounced* ***clean*** *perfume reminiscent of grape skins.*	*Lots of acidity; shortage of mouth-filling fruit.*	*Typical example of good modern white winemaking with low-temperature fermentation, but a bit short of character. Won't improve.*
St Véran 1978 Louis Jadot, Mâconnais	*Pale yellow.*	*Great 'green fruit' attraction.*	*Perfect balance between acidity and pure Chardonnay fruit and body.*	*Tastes much more youthful than a 1978 because of pronounced acid, but already drinking well.*
Château Giscours 1979 Cru Classé, Margaux	*Concentrated crimson (very like the 1978 tasted alongside).*	*Warm, rich, oaky – almost like a California Cabernet.*	*Very powerful. Tannin very evident still, but not overwhelming.*	*Claret with a great future. Better than many other 1979s tasted and should mature within the decade.*
Wynns Coonawarra Cabernet Sauvignon 1978 South Australia	*Great 'legs'. Blackish crimson. Lighter than average for Australian Cabernet.*	*Some blackcurrant character together with lots of extract.*	*A heavyweight. Warm-climate soft Cabernet with flavour fading to a short finish.*	*More elegant than many Coonawarra Cabernets but still not for the faint-hearted. Almost mature.*
Bernkasteler Doktor Beerenauslese 1971 Estate bottled by Deinhard, Middle Mosel	*Dark, syrupy gold with tawny tinge.*	*Burnt petroly nose. Some acid evident already. Slightly musty at first.*	*Very sweet at the front of the mouth but a dry finish. Layer upon layer of honeyed flavour during and after each mouthful.*	*Wonderful mature rich Riesling. A great treat. Glad I wasn't paying!*

* *Entries in this column tend to be a confirmation of the flavour as initially sensed by the nose, together with notes on the cruder dimensions such as sweetness, acidity, tannin, body.*

descriptions of each aspect of the wine's full assault on the senses, usually categorized as shown opposite. (Conclusions should probably be headed 'Brain'.) When starting out, it helps to be wordy rather than terse, so that you establish what sort of characteristics you normally associate with various groups of wines. As you get more experienced you can begin to omit the features you've come to expect and note only the most striking aspects of the wine.

Make sure that glasses aren't too thimble-like

If you do most of your tasting in a fairly structured way, usually at home and occasionally out with like-minded friends, you could keep all your tasting notes in one book. Such a written record of your drinking experience, if you persevere and taste a sufficiently wide range, you might find to be extremely valuable one day. Looseleaf binders are useful for those who taste more peripatetically, and those who enjoy fiddling about with cards and coloured pens could even develop a wonderful system of cross-referencing their tastings by type of wine. 'Now let's see. . .when did I last taste Louis Latour's Meursault?' A simple flick through an immaculate card index and you'd find notes on the 1979 to compare with the 1981 in front of you. What a *coup*. And of course the micro-chip opens up all sorts of possibilities.

Wines change with age so do try to date your tasting notes.

And when reaching conclusions about a wine take into account some assessment of how ready for drinking you think it is (the amount of tannin in red wines, and acid in whites, is a good pointer here) as well as how good it is. There is more on assessing wines below.

The noble art of spitting

It's heartbreaking but true: there are no tasting faculties in your throat, so you don't *need* to swallow wine to taste it. In fact, the less you swallow, the less clouded your perceptions will be by the haze of alcohol and the better you will be able to taste. You may think that only after you swallow a wine do you get a proper perception of its aftertaste. But that's not taste, it's an after*glow* – the simple and none-too-subtle effect of ethyl alcohol. If you spit out every mouthful, you will be amazed at how your tasting notes stay legible longer.

Take a mouthful of wine, taste it as instructed so far – monitoring its effects on your mouth and brain – and then spit it out. Compare the sensation with that of monitoring the mouthful and then swallowing it. Is there really any difference in taste? Okay, swallowing the wine might leave a few more volatiles at the back of your mouth, well placed to waft up the retro-nasal passage, but the difference is marginal. Notice how fully you can experience the 'finish' of a wine even if you spit it out.

I am not suggesting that you expectorate on social occasions. In fact, spitting out good wine seems as much a waste to me as it doubtless does to you. There are, however, some circumstances in which it is wise to spit out the alcohol, if possible.

★ When you want to keep sober, either because you're driving or because of other commitments after the tasting.
★ When you're tasting a dauntingly high number of wines, more than half a dozen, say.
★ When you're tasting very young wines that don't give a great deal of pleasure, and you are not in need of alcohol.

Just a word of warning. Even if you carefully spit out every single mouthful, you will probably not escape entirely the effects of alcohol. Come what may, alcoholic fumes will travel around your mouth, up your nose and retro-nasal passage, and you may feel slightly light headed. In any case, you will find it extremely difficult not to swallow a single drop of wine – and all those fumes will further prejudice the results of a breathalyser. Because of their profession, French wine brokers are said to get special dispensation from 'l'alcotest'.

Losing inhibitions about spitting in

Practise spitting neatly in the bath.

public is one of the first things to be done by the embryonic wine taster. It is sad but irrefutable that wine, that wonderfully intriguing and uplifting liquid, contains a potentially dangerous substance. When it makes sense to spit, you should be proud rather than ashamed to do it. You may associate expectoration with rather seedy old men and pavements, but wine people have perfected the art of doing it with great style. 'Spit with pride' might well be the wine taster's motto. The stylish spit is forceful, an elegant trajectory with not the merest suggestion of a dribble, aimed dead centre of the spittoon.

Put lots of force behind each spit, purse your lips and aim for your feet. You are not expected to spit in silence.

Practice spitting in the bath

Any old jug can earn itself the smart appellation of spittoon, though to avoid nasty splashes it makes sense to put some absorber like torn paper or sawdust into the bottom of it. A wooden wine case, such as those used by the better Bordeaux châteaux, filled with sawdust is a smart spittoon, though a spittoon with running water is even more efficient at disposing of the unsavoury evidence. If you can taste near a suitable sink then the business of spitting is easy.

Formal tastings

Here is a brief description of a clinically formal tasting so that you'll know what to do if invited to one, or want to organize a particularly pukka wine tasting for friends.

Up to one hundred wines may be 'on show', though most tasters tackle

You will probably find that the number of different wines you can

only about thirty of them. An open bottle of each is set out on long tables covered with white tablecloths. If the organizer has been thoughtful, the tables will be sufficiently well spaced to allow good traffic flow. Spittoons should, similarly, be strategically placed. Many's the time I've spent most of a tasting with cheeks bulging as I jostle my way through the crowd to the lone spittoon in the far corner. There may be the odd jug of water to rinse glasses or palates, and some edible but not too distracting blotting paper in the form of low-flavour savoury biscuits. Carr's Table Water are fine, Bath Olivers show real style and little cubes of (English) cheese are likely to flatter the wines.

Spittoons should be placed strategically

In most circumstances, even at the dinner table, there is a conventional order in which wines are served or tasted, and it makes quite a bit of sense. 'White before red, dry before sweet and young before old' encapsulates it. As with serving-temperature considerations, 'white before red' is really a loose way of

study seriously in one session will increase steadily and then reach a maximum – quite literally, saturation point. I would suggest that you start by comparing only two wines. The first exercise in specific wine tasting, contrasting two Chablis of different qualities, is a good starting point. Quite soon you will find you are able to look in detail at three wines, still getting enjoyment out of them without feeling overwhelmed.

The bigger the group in which you taste, the more wines you can afford to tackle. You'll probably find, though, that twelve at a time are the absolute maximum. Many professionals try to limit themselves to even fewer, although I know the odd wine authority who seems to have infinite resistance to acid and alcohol and can still write a wonderfully neat tasting-note on wine number 113 (the greatest number I've ever seen tackled at one time – and they were all 1979 Beaujolais from a single producer, marathon-man Duboeuf).
Try chewing a dry biscuit between mouthfuls of wine and notice how little it seems to affect the palate. Now try a mouthful of Cheddar and see how a fairly substantial red wine seems to give you just the taste you want to complement the cheese flavour.

When planning what wines to serve with a meal (if it's the sort of occasion that warrants more than one wine), bear in mind the conventional sequence of wines. For more on this (actually very uncomplicated) subject, see Chapter 6, 'Wine, food and fun'.

saying 'light bodied before full bodied', so that a wine is never overwhelmed by one that preceded it. It makes sense not to put dry wines at a disadvantage by coating your mouth with sweetness first (though the French almost always serve something sweet as an aperitif and somehow seem to survive). The older a wine, in general, the more fascinating it is (true only of fine wine, though – don't try 'maturing' a cheap *vin de table*). It is therefore sensible to ascend to a peak of quality as a tasting climax.

At a tasting organized by a wine merchant, the choice of wines will be dictated by those he wants to sell to you. If you're organizing a tasting, you might well follow some of the suggested exercises in this course. Any tasting organized around a grape variety is always fascinating. It is relatively easy to find examples of, say, the Cabernet Sauvignon from all over the world, and by tasting each one you can learn a lot not only about that varietal but about the regions where they were made.

You could also taste the range of wines made by a single producer, to try to come to grips with each of them and his particular style. Some of the most fascinating and intellectual tasting exercises, however, are based on either a 'horizontal' or 'vertical' tasting. Tasting horizontally has nothing to do with reclining on Recamier couches but involves studying lots of similar but different wines of the same vintage – all of the 1978 Pauillacs, for example, to see how Château Latour 1978 compares with

You don't have to be a millionaire to indulge in one of these 'directional' tastings. Bordeaux's rather formal structure of ranked châteaux lends itself particularly well to the technique, but the wines don't have to be 'premiers crus'. Any collection of wines from a single vintage, no matter how humble the château or blended Claret, can give you a horizontal tasting, and will teach you something about that vintage.

You can attempt a vertical tasting of any wine with a vintage date on the label – though it might take quite

Châteaux Lafite and Mouton-Rothschild. Tasting vertically involves tasting different vintages of the same wine; vintages of Château Latour 1982 back to 1970, for example.

At a formal tasting you will usually be given your own tasting glass and be expected to make do with a fairly small tasting sample, up to an inch deep, of each wine, emptying any remains into a large 'dregs' jug or bottle with a funnel before starting on the next wine. Sometimes, if wines or glasses are in very short supply, there'll be a single glass of each wine placed in front of its bottle for everyone to taste from. I think any disease would have to be very rabid to manage to transmit itself from one taster to another via a glass rinsed in wine – alcohol being a strong disinfectant. If tasting as cosily as this, though, it really does make a bit of a stink if you leave the smell of cigarette smoke or perfume on the glass.

a bit of scouting about to gather together much of a collection of different vintages. Most wine merchants sell, at best, two recent vintages of a given wine and only a handful can offer a good range of mature vintages. Try these mature wine sources:

Adnams of Southwold
Averys of Bristol
Berry Bros & Rudd, London SW1
Corney & Barrow, London EC1
Fields, London SW3
Gerard Harris of Aston Clinton
Harrods, London SW1
Justerini & Brooks, London SW1
Luc Lacerre, Cardiff
Lay & Wheeler, Colchester
Laytons, London NW1
Milroy's, London W1
Reid Wines, Hallatrow, Bristol
La Réserve, London SW3
Henry Townsend, Amersham
La Vigneronne, London SW7
The Wine Society, Stevenage

Tasting 'blind'

Organizing a 'blind' tasting is quite a lot of work, though the amount you learn can make it very rewarding. It is absolutely staggering how important a part the label plays in the business of tasting. If we know that a favourite region, producer or vintage is coming up, we automatically start relishing it – giving it every benefit of the tasting doubt. It took me five years of annual disappointing and puzzling blind Champagne tastings before I realized that I didn't actually like the

The simplest way to 'mask' bottles (if they're shaped identically) is to wrap them in tin foil or to adopt the American technique of 'brown-bagging' them. For this, you need a collection of fairly tough opaque paper bags into which you can pack each bottle, either taping the bags closed round the neck or simply scrunching the paper up tightly. Remember to take all the capsules off completely so that there aren't any distracting identification signals. You'll need to give each bottle a taste of Bollinger, as much as its ethos and label.

You will need to ensure that no clues to identity are given. This may mean painstakingly decanting every wine into a set of anonymous bottles (the standard green Claret one is fairly easy to collect), though this would not be suitable for very delicate wines. Otherwise, you will have to employ one of the bottle-disguise methods outlined on these pages.

If you really get the wine bug, you may want to let the bug eat into your social life by serving wines blind when entertaining. (It's easier then, because you can use decanters or a well-placed hand when pouring the bottle.) This can be great fun if everyone is equally interested in, and equipped for, making a guess. It can also be extremely tedious, especially if you refuse to give any clues or encouragement. Be wary of torturing your guests.

number or a letter, either scribbled on the bag or swinging round the neck on a reusable cardboard label. Oh, and if you're using foil, it is of course much easier to open the bottles after wrapping, so the sequence should be: de-capsule, wrap, open, number, taste, panic.

Australia's most vocal wine man, Len Evans, has devised a more socially acceptable variation on the guessing theme. In his Options Game the host starts by asking of his wine: 'Is it Bordeaux or Burgundy?' Even if you get that wrong, you can all go on to the next question: 'Is it Médoc/Graves or St Emilion/Pomerol?' The Australians are so sharp they actually start at the next level of question, 'Pauillac or Margaux?' The host might then go on to, 'Is it pre- or post-1974?', '1976, 1975 or 1979?' And finally, 'Château Palmer, Issan or Lascombes?' All pretty tricky stuff, but it's a game that everyone can play right to the end.

Assessing quality

Blind tasting may be a fairly rarefied and not terribly useful skill, but some guidance on assessing a wine's quality can help you enjoy just a bit more every wine that comes your way.

This is particularly beneficial because price is no direct indicator of quality. There is no great wine

Top quality Vouvray is hard to find in this country. O. W. Loeb of Jermyn Street, London SW1, lists

available at £2.50 a bottle (though there is still some on sale for less than £5 and it's often called Vouvray). There are, on the other hand, some very disappointing wines that cost more than £5 a bottle, and there is an enormous variation in the quality of wines currently on sale for between £2.50 and £5. So it makes sense to learn how to judge quality in an educated and rational way.

The two most obvious pointers to quality – balance and length – have already been outlined on page 37. You can enjoy a fairly basic wine, such as a Muscadet or a Beaujolais, if it's well made. Look for the sensation in your mouth after you have swallowed or spat out a mouthful of the wine, as well as monitoring its flavour and how complex it is. A fine example of a Meursault or a Barolo is likely to be an obviously 'greater' wine, with more layers of flavour and intrigue, but there is a time and place for every sort of wine. There have been one or two periods of my life when I have been lucky enough to taste nothing but great wines for days on end. I wouldn't say it was pure hell, but by the end this ungrateful wretch was aching for a simple glass of something straightforward and everyday. We need variety in wine drinking as much as in anything else. Don't think that's it's not worth learning about wine if you can't afford to spend more than a few pounds a month on it. There is good and bad quality at every price level.

To concentrate your mind on assessing the quality of a wine it helps to give it a score, as well as making the usual tasting notes on it.

those of Foreau and, as I write, has a 1967 Demi Sec at £4.99.

To find disappointing wines costing well over £5 a bottle (though you are unlikely to be that keen) you would be well advised to make a speciality of red Burgundy. See the section on Pinot Noir for specific names that can be trusted in this minefield of quality.

It helps to give the wine a score

Some tasters score out of ten, some out of twenty, some out of five and some even out of seven. I find I need twenty points to allocate, and even

This is particularly helpful if you're tasting a range of similar wines with a view to picking out your favourites. After all, one of the chief consequences of informal comparative tasting should be to note the names of those wines, producers and vintages that give you particular pleasure.

Funnily enough, likes and dislikes, the one area everyone who doesn't know much about wine does invariably proclaim they know about, tend to recede with the gaining of knowledge and experience of wine (sounds much grander than just drinking it, doesn't it?). Most professional tasters end up with more or less the same concept of what makes a good wine.

Happy tasting.

then I find myself tempted into halves. The twenty-point scale is the one most often used by official judging panels and other medal-awarders. Practise adding a score to the conclusions in your tasting-notes. The most common problem with scoring is deciding whether to score an immature wine for current pleasure or its potential quality. You may have to invent your own symbol here. My tasting-notes are often littered with arrows to show likely future development.

Another problem with scoring and assessment is more philosophical. If you're tasting a wine that gives you great pleasure and yet doesn't seem to you a typical example of what it's supposed to be, how should you score it? Very much an A-level question this, but one that might provide the subject of a post-tasting debate. And, you will find, the discussion afterwards is one of wine tasting's greatest pleasures.

You will find the discussion of wine afterwards one of life's great pleasures

3 The raw material – white grapes

First know your grape

Curiously, only one sort of wine actually tastes like grapes, and that is wine made from Muscat or related grape varieties.

'Nose' any of the following wines and notice how like the taste of Muscat grapes they smell. 'Grapey' might be your first tasting note: Asti Spumante; Moscato; Spanish Muscatel; Moscatel de Setubal; any southern French Muscat from, say, Beaumes de Venise, Rivesaltes or Banyuls; Muscat d'Alsace. Arm yourself with a few grapes and a glass of wine to sip. Contrast the two flavours.

In every other case, wine tastes quite different from grapes, even from those grapes from which it was made. Grapes have a simple fruity flavour, their lack of deviousness having caused wine folk to label it 'rather one-dimensional'. Wine on the other hand has a much more complicated taste, definitely two-, possibly even three-dimensional. There are layers of flavour here, different nuances, though underneath everything there should be the same basic fruitiness that grapes have. The winemaker's job is to transform his raw material, grapes, into something as interesting as wine, while retaining their common attribute, fruitiness.

Grape skins taste astringent. The pips when crushed taste bitter. Only the flesh, which is mainly juice, is suitable raw material for a fresh, fruity white wine. (Red wines may need a bit of astringency or tannin – see page 26.) The first stage in making a white wine therefore is to

Peel yourself a grape. Taste the flesh. Then chew the peel, and nibble a pip. These last two exercises are an uncommonly unpleasant part of this wine course.

eliminate the skin and pips from the process by gently crushing the grapes and running off the juice. The harder the grapes are pressed the more astringency the resultant wine will pick up from the skins. Fine white wines are made from 'the free-run juice', i.e. the juice that can be drained from a vat of grapes crushed by their own weight. In an area where a wine earns its right to an appellation by virtue of the grape type and where it was grown (e.g. most of France), cheaper versions often contain a high proportion of juice from very hard pressed grapes.

Contrast the flavours of a good Chablis from a reputable producer such as Drouhin, Michel, Albert Pic, and a cheap generic Chablis bottled in the UK.

The juice contains sugar because the grapes were ripe and this can now be fermented into alcohol, turning sweet grape juice into a much drier liquid that can be called wine. (This is why grape juice is always sweet. The only way to get it 'drier' is to ferment out the sugar. Those who insist on tinkering about with nature, and humanity's naturally greedy instincts, may sometimes then de-alcoholize the wine so that they may have dry grape juice.)

Yeast is the stuff that converts the sugar to alcohol. Yeasts occur naturally in the 'bloom' on grape skins (and are therefore mixed into the juice) in any established vineyard; or cultured yeasts may be introduced for even greater control over the process. When they've done their work they die, so wines very rarely taste 'yeasty'.

Peel a black grape and a white grape ***(— page 102)***

This fermented grape juice is now wine although, as demonstrated below, it is capable of extraordinary variation of taste.

Gewürztraminer – the most recognizable grape

Gewürztraminer may be one of the most difficult grape varieties to pronounce (Guh-*vurts*-trah-mee-ner) and spell, but it is probably the easiest to imprint on your palate memory for future recognition. It has a heady, almost perfumed, lychee scent. Some find it reminiscent of tropical fruit, without being too certain of which one. There's something definitely exotic about Gewürz (which is German for 'spiced', a fairly accurate description), though it can pall after a while. Connoisseurs claim to find it too obvious – a bit like scented cachous – after prolonged exposure to it, but it's a wonderful safe starting point for the wine taster.

The 'traminer' bit of its name is derived from the village of Tramin in the Italian Tyrol, and there are still some light, delicate Gewürztraminers made in the hills of north-east Italy. Most Gewürztraminer found in Britain, however, is from Alsace on the Franco-German border. Alsace is famous for its perfumed wines, which smell sweetish but actually taste dry (providing the exception to prove the rule that the palate usually merely confirms what the nose already suspected). Alsace Gewürztraminers are a force to be reckoned with as they ripen well, but all the sugar in the grapes is fermented out to make a dry wine high in alcohol, often as much as 13%. They smell lusciously pungent but have a dry finish. The grapes themselves are unusual in that many of them are pinkish, not white at all,

Examine an Alsace Gewürztraminer from a recent vintage. Léon Beyer are renowned for their very rich Gewürz, Trimbach make a very crisp one, and Hugel are dependable. Sainsbury's usually stock their own keenly priced example. Note the curious perfume and try to come up with your own description of it: lychees, mangoes, cachous? Notice how it suggests sweetness on the nose but is then followed by a dry but full-bodied taste. Try a bit on the tip of your tongue to test sweetness. Contrast the very powerful distinctive nose with that of a basic dry white table wine. Almost any other white wine will seem a very shy little flower indeed beside the orchid-like Gewürz.

Very few German Gewürztraminers find their way to Britain, but Lenz Moser have sent some impressive Austrian sweet examples which have been available from Les Amis du Vin of London W12, and on request from Victoria Wine. Note the rich golden colour, even in youngish examples, and the thick, almost oily texture. A number of California Gewürz have been shipped here, as well as one rather impressive one from Associated Vintners in Seattle, Washington State. Grand Cru of Sonoma has made California's most acclaimed. The grape is also grown in Yugoslavia, and one of the cheapest ways of tasting it is via Victoria Wine's Traminer, a rather coarse, flabby wine but with definite spicy Traminer characteristics in its aroma. Seek out examples of Gewürztraminer and note what they and Gewürz can sometimes be quite a deep-coloured straw yellow. Low acidity is characteristic of Gewürztraminer made in a fairly warm climate, and some of them go rather 'oily' with age.

In Gewürztraminer's homeland, Alsace, it's considered a very noble but rather tiring grape, and the winemakers themselves often prefer to drink Riesling. It is also grown across the Rhine in the warmish German wine regions of Rheinpfalz or the Palatinate, Rheinhessen and Baden (where it's usually left quite sweet), and in Austria where it can make delicious, deep golden, very sweet dessert wines. There has been considerable experimentation with the variety in California, where wines are never quite as dry as in Alsace and can sometimes be as sweet as Austria's sweetest. Italian Gewürz is the most underplayed. Some Gewürztraminers may be labelled simply Traminer.

The only possible taste confusion may be with the grapey Muscat, as both are very aromatic and have a sweet, flowery smell.

all have in common. Even light Gewürztraminers from Italy and New Zealand have that funny smell. Try to establish firmly your own palate picture of the varietal.

Gewürztraminer may be one of the most difficult grape varieties to pronounce

A-level: if you get the chance, try to taste a Gewürztraminer alongside a Muscat. The most revealing pair would come from the same Alsace producer and should reveal the added richness, spice and lesser grapiness that Gewürz has, compared with Muscat.

Sauvignon and what sunshine does

Sauvignon Blanc is another very distinctive grape variety and has great appeal for those who appreciate crisp, dry, uncomplicated wines. The cartons of empty Sancerre and Pouilly-Fumé bottles collected from restaurants all over the world every morning testify to that. It is grown in all sorts of different wine regions, which is why I have chosen it to

To get to grips with the essential Sauvignon-ness of Sauvignon you could not do better than start with a Sancerre or Pouilly-Fumé from a good grower. Yapp Bros, of Mere in Wiltshire, could supply either, and the wines of Baron Patrick de Ladoucette or the rather more earthy Jean Vacheron are irreproachable. (These last two belong to that illustrate the effect of climate on taste, but there is not too much variation in its distinctive aroma. 'Cats' pee on a gooseberry bush' may not sound a very appealing description to you, but after a bit of exposure to, and consideration of, the smell, you may come round to agreeing with it. There's something very definitely 'green' about the smell; some people find raw gooseberries, others the smell of blackcurrant leaves. Just to smell the wine gets you ready for the whack of acidity with which it will cut the palate, and perhaps that is what has earned it the loose but evocative adjective 'flinty'. You're supposed to get a whiff of gunsmoke from a good Pouilly-Fumé and, indeed, as a ready victim of auto-suggestion, I often have, though I've never smelt actual gunsmoke. This is what tasting notes are all about – finding terms that match flavours most closely, even if only imagined.

Sauvignon is a grape made for our times, times of high interest rates. The wines should be drunk while they're young and fresh. Choose the youngest vintage available, for the grape's fruit is not the opulent sort that develops intriguing complexity with age. It simply gets a bit stale and the initially high acidity starts to predominate. The wines are usually very pale straw in colour, except in the rare (and expensive) examples that have been given a period in wood, and have taken on a golden tinge. Acidity is the most pronounced characteristic of the wines and almost all are dry to bone dry. There will rarely be any great length of flavour, which tends to tail off swiftly after a rather dashing

infuriating class of top-quality French wines that are easier to find on restaurant wine lists than on the shelf.) Sauvignon de St Bris, from Harveys of Pall Mall and Bristol, and Sauvignon de Haut-Poitou, available from Lay & Wheeler of Colchester, are also good clean examples.

Try to establish your own trigger words for the grape. Green fruit? Herbaceous? Gooseberries? Flinty? I find that a helpful way to recognize Sauvignon is first to realize that it hits your senses in a very direct way, so that it's 'pointed' along the middle of your mouth and nose rather than having a much broader fan-like flavour like that of Gewürztraminer or the Chardonnay examined below.

A-level: very much an optional-extra tasting at this stage, but good examples of the richness that a bit of Sémillon can give to the slightly lean flavour of the Sauvignon are Robert Mondavi's Fumé Blanc and Joseph Phelps' Sauvignon Blanc from start. Some Californian and very smart Bordeaux producers blend in a bit of the Sémillon grape (see page 87) to give more weight and a longer-lasting flavour. Without this palate-filler Sémillon, Sauvignon is light to medium bodied.

The Loire Valley is the coolest place where Sauvignon is cultivated, and Loire Sauvignons will either be labelled with the grape name or with that of one of the Sauvignon-producing appellations such as Sancerre, Pouilly-Fumé, Quincy, Reuilly or Menetou-Salon. Sauvignon de St Bris, made in the far north of Burgundy, also demonstrates the cool climate style of Sauvignon that's dry, very acid and almost steely, it's so pure and tart. Sauvignon is also responsible for most dry white Bordeaux; the more temperate climate there on the Atlantic seaboard can be 'tasted' in the slightly less acidic, more open wines. Sauvignons from Yugoslavia also demonstrate how a bit more sunshine cuts down the acidity you can taste in a wine. The Sauvignons and Fumé Blancs of California show what happens when you transplant the varietal to a positively warm climate. The nearer the Equator any sort of grapes are grown and ripened, the less acid and more sugar there will be in the resulting must, and the less acid and more sugar or alcohol there will be in the wine – unless deliberate steps are taken, such as picking the grapes unusually early. This was already hinted at by the different examples of Gewürztraminer examined above; those made in the hotter climate of Austria have noticeably less acid than the Alsace versions.

California (try Les Amis du Vin, of London W12, Harrods, and La Vigneronne, London SW7); also, from Bordeaux, Château Laville-Haut-Brion and, more affordably, Domaine de Chevalier and Château Carbonnieux.

Now try to contrast Sauvignons grown in different climates. One of the wines mentioned above would be fine as your coolest representative, or a Sauvignon de Touraine from the middle Loire would be cheaper and still noticeably acid and dry (if a little less pure in flavour). A dry white Bordeaux would make a good example of a temperate-climate Sauvignon. An increasing proportion of such wines are now sold with the word Sauvignon on the label, though the French have been much less concerned to specify grape varieties than winemakers in newer wine regions such as California and Australia. There's a Sauvignon Sec from Delor that is fairly well distributed, but almost any white Bordeaux in a green straight-sided bottle (often called Château Something) would provide an example of the looser, rather less acid, style of a Sauvignon that has been ripened by a bit more sunshine. Cheaper (and, sorry, coarser) would be Victoria Wine's Yugoslav Sauvignon from Fruska Gora. This wine tastes almost sweet and demonstrates nicely the lower acids in a warmer-climate wine.

Most Sauvignons from California (where the clever Robert Mondavi revitalized the sales appeal of the varietal in the early 1970s by re-naming it Fumé Blanc) are noticeably different from their cousins reared in

Of course, climate is only one of the many factors that affect the taste of wine. The differences you will taste in any range of Sauvignons could in part be attributed to things like their age, the age of the vines themselves, winemaking techniques or even the exact clone of the vine planted. (American Sauvignon always tastes distinctly more flowery than French to me and this may be the explanation.) We will be examining all these factors, but at this point try to concentrate purely on the softening effect of sunshine. What happened to the grapes can be tasted in the wine, whether it's a Sauvignon Blanc or any other grape variety. The more acid a wine is the less sunshine is likely to have ripened the grapes, and the cooler the climate it is likely to have come from.

chillier France. 'Grassy' is the word that lots of Californians associate with the varietal, and it certainly produces rather more florid wines over there. They are rarely bone dry and are noticeably different on the nose and tip of the tongue from cool-climate Sauvignons. Gallo export an inexpensive but representative west-coast ambassador across the Atlantic, and it has been stocked by Oddbins and The Wine Studio, SW1. A similar 'warmer' wine is sent across the Atlantic from Chile by the Spanish wine firm Torres, which has a South American outpost there producing inexpensive white Sauvignon-based Santa Digna. South Africa is now also producing some relatively rich examples of warm-climate Sauvignon Blanc. Collison's of London SW1 should stock at least one good example.

Chardonnay and the kiss of oak

Unlike Sauvignon Blanc and Gewürztraminer, which are designed primarily for a giddy youth, Chardonnay is a grape that produces wines capable of doing wonderful things in their middle and old age. Only the Riesling is a serious rival to Chardonnay's claim to be the greatest white grape in the world. Montrachet, which has its home in Burgundy, has done quite a bit for Chardonnay's reputation in the past. However, dazzling Chardonnays emerging from some of the world's newer wine regions are doing their bit to reinforce the glamour that surrounds the variety. It's capable of a wider variation of flavour and

To form a satisfactory impression of Chardonnay you will probably have to taste it in three forms: youthful and carefree, mature and fascinating, and warm-hearted and rich. For the first, a good white Mâcon will do nicely. Georges Duboeuf makes fine examples of St Véran, Pouilly-Fuissé and Pouilly-Vinzelles, and his wines are stocked by Davisons and Gough Brothers. This is the most straightforward and affordable way of experiencing the positive, smoky flavour of the Chardonnay, which at this early stage in its development has something a bit 'appley' about it. I'm always reminded of melons by a good Mâcon Blanc.

quality than either of the varieties examined so far, but is characterized by being dry, full-bodied and with a much 'broader' flavour than pointed, edgy Sauvignon. You can feel the weight of the wine immediately and know that this is no beguilingly aromatic aperitif, but a meaty, almost beefy, number that demands attention. Because of this weight and firmness, the acidity of a Chardonnay is not usually as noticeable as in the lighter-bodied Sauvignon. But, however opulent the Chardonnay seems to taste, it is always dry. Admittedly the richer California Chardonnays hover towards the brink of medium dryness because they're so alcoholic, but the grape is fundamentally designed for dry wines. (The only Chardonnay I have ever tasted that had been specially vinified to produce a sweet wine was really rather unpleasantly flat.)

The second style of Chardonnay is to my mind the finest, though it is very much a high-day-or-holiday sort of purchase. At least dependably fine white Burgundy is easier to find than fine red wine from Burgundy's heartland, the Côte d'Or, and few bottles of Meursault, Montrachet and Corton Charlemagne are likely to disappoint. Louis Latour's and Bonneau de Martray's Corton Charlemagne, Domaine Leflaive's Montrachets and Marquis de Laguiche Montrachet represent pinnacles in the Chardonnay landscape. To appreciate what they really have to give, treat yourself to one that's at least five and preferably fifteen years old. These wines have accumulated so much flavour they demand rapt attention. Don't serve them with food that will spoil as it cools – and remember to serve all Chardonnays a bit warmer than most white wines because of their weight. In fact these are the wines that could be mistaken for red; they're so long they could cure a sore throat. 'Steely' and 'meaty' might both be used here.

California or Australia is the obvious source of the third kind of Chardonnay, the sort that's just bursting out of itself with flavour. Almost all such wines will state alcohol content on the label, as European wines will have to do eventually. Choose one that's at least 13.5° and, even if it is a youthful example, you will probably be rewarded with a very luscious, deep yellow, almost viscous liquid that tastes of a rather exotic fruit salad and is so rich it's almost sweet.

Somewhere floating around these three wines, in the flavour you absorb chiefly through your nose, is

To form your palate picture of Chardonnay you will probably need to taste more examples of it than were necessary to come to grips with the more obvious Gewürztraminer or Sauvignon, but a certain 'smokiness' in the bouquet of any Chardonnay is, for me, the grape's chief distinguishing mark. Another very revealing characteristic of Chardonnay is that, unlike the two varietals studied so far, its flavour seems to gain intensity in the mouth. Any well-made example will have a fascinating long finish that may seem more powerful than the initial bouquet.

Chardonnay is traditionally thought to reach its apogee on the Côte d'Or, the heartland of the Burgundy region, in wines such as Corton-Charlemagne, the Montrachets and some Meursaults. Not quite as great, but still good, white Burgundies can be found lurking behind labels saying Pernand-Vergelesses, Auxey-Duresses, St Aubin, Rully, Montagny and Bourgogne Blanc. From the southern, less smart, end of Burgundy come Chardonnays called St Véran, Pouillys of all sorts except Pouilly-Fumé, Beaujolais Blanc and Mâcon Blanc. None of these will actually say Chardonnay

what Chardonnay is all about. My word is 'smoky' because Chardonnay seems almost to catch my throat, perhaps in anticipation of the spread of flavours that will constitute the finish of the wine somewhere in that vicinity, in contrast to the solely nasal appreciation of aromatic varieties like Gewürztraminer and Sauvignon. As it mellows, it takes on so much richness that it's almost 'buttery'.

To get some idea of the full range that the Chardonnay grape can offer, you could start at the most basic level with a Bulgarian example, Hatch Mansfield's Le Chouan produced in the Loire, or the Italian Le Rugiade from Les Amis du Vin, London W12. These are unadorned wines made for early consumption, with only the faintest suggestion of Chardonnay flavour. Just up the scale, from the same areas respectively and still well below £4 a bottle, are the Chardonnay de Haut Poitou from Caves de la Madeleine, London SW10, and (another Italian one) Santa Margherita from Findlaters, London W1. With the Mâcons and Pouillys suggested above, these represent the best-value way of tasting the pure fruit flavour of Chardonnay.

For more exotic Chardonnay-based wines, seek out: German Weissburgunder specimens from the German Food Centre; Gran Viña Sol from Torres stockists; the lovely golden Australian Chardonnays of Tyrrell's from Averys of Bristol and from Brown Bros from W. H. Cullen; or put yourself at the mercy of the eclectic La Vigneronne of London SW7. Note that the most luscious and full-bodied examples on the label; nor will the only other two French wines that are traditionally based on Chardonnay – Chablis, made sixty miles north of the Côte d'Or, and Champagne. Most Champagnes contain about one third Chardonnay grapes, and those called Blanc de Blancs are made of nothing but. If you want to taste a still wine made from Chardonnay grown in the Champagne region, look for a Coteaux Champenois Blanc de Blancs.

come from the warmest regions, as was demonstrated with Sauvignons.

Because the rewards can be so great, Chardonnay has been taken from its home base in north-eastern France and cultivated all over the world; and such wines will normally be more easily identifiable, with Chardonnay specified – nay boasted – on the label. Chardonnay has been an enormous success in California and Australia; they're winding themselves up to a similar peak in South Africa and New Zealand; it's all the rage in Italy now; and there are plantings from Catalonia to Lebanon, from Chile to New York State.

The flavour of any Chardonnay evolves considerably with maturation, and the most influential factor here is whether the wine is given any time in wood. Chardonnay and oak seem made for each other, and many winemakers with serious aspirations for their Chardonnays (and the cash to buy and maintain barrels) try to give them a bit of wood ageing. Sometimes, to add on a new layer of oak flavour, even the fermenting is done in oak rather than the more neutral stainless steel or other inert substance used in the 'fresh fruit' technique of fermenting which emphasizes the fruitiness of the grapes.

To get some idea of what oak ageing does to the taste of wine, arm yourself with a bottle of Chablis (perhaps the same trusty one as has already been used in two previous exercises). O. W. Loeb, of London SW1, stock the archetypal no-wood Chablis of Louis Michel. This represents Chardonnay at its purest and least adorned by the influence either of oak or of prolonged sunshine. There's a lean fruit flavour here that is almost steely. Its impact on the palate, if it's a youthful example high in acidity, can be close to pain – so dry is the wine. It is something like Sauvignon, except that the flavour doesn't have that

Wines of any sort, red or white, that have been kept in wood definitely taste different, especially if that wood is fairly new (or newly shaved) with lots of oak flavour still to give, and if the barrels are small so that the wood-to-wine ratio is relatively high. As we shall see, wines such as Rioja and young Claret demonstrate very well the effect of wood ageing on red wines, but Chardonnay provides the best examples of how well wood and white wine can work together. A whole new range of flavours are introduced to make the wine much more complicated and rewarding, but they need time to meld together and produce a balanced wine. That's why wood ageing makes most sense for wines destined for a longish life. There would be no point in giving Sancerre a year in small oak casks as it's a wine that is made expressly to be enjoyed young and fresh – from the Sauvignon grape, which doesn't age well.

In the recesses of our subconscious, most of us probably associate wooden casks more with traditional winemakers than with those in what we rather patronizingly call the New World. Ironically, however, as an ever-higher proportion of Chardonnay made in France is denied the chance of lodging in oak, it is the Californians in particular who have been frantically shipping casks across the Atlantic from top French coopers to give added richness to their Chardonnays. Only a handful of Chablis producers, for instance, have any wood in their cellars, while most Napa and Sonoma wineries are stacked high with expensive barrels. Some of the

aromatic edge of cats'-pee but hints at something broader.

At the other end of the scale of oakiness would be a California Chardonnay from a producer such as Robert Mondavi, Cuvaison, Firestone and Joseph Phelps. These wines gain a sweetish, almost vanilla-like overlay of oaky flavours together with a golden hue and considerable weight; so much that it can sometimes be confused with sweetness. These wines are so rich that you may find them difficult to drink throughout a meal, though vintages after 1978 are likely to be less pronounced. For wines with this obvious oaky character, try Les Amis du Vin of London W12, Averys of Bristol, La Vigneronne of London SW7, or even the less expensive examples of California Chardonnay stocked by Sainsbury's, Victoria Wine and Peter Dominic.

A-level: If you wish to progress to greater subtleties, you should try to pick out the much more subdued oakiness of the example of great Côte d'Or Burgundy you selected at the start of this Chardonnay exercise. Leflaive, Louis Latour and Joseph Drouhin (for Marquis de Laguiche) all use some oak barrels in the ageing of their top wines, but it is usually evident only in a suggestion of vanilla on the nose and a very slight deepening of colour (sometimes also a certain buttery flavour). Harrods, Gerard Harris of Aston Clinton, and Lay & Wheeler of Colchester might be able to supply wines of this quality.

S-level: And now for real enthusiasts,

new enthusiasts have rather overdone the oak, and we have seen a spate of Chardonnays weighed down not only by alcohol but also by all the rich flavours associated with oak and the marriage between oak and wine. Some of them can be enjoyable, if only in small quantities, and they certainly provide a superb opportunity to taste what 'oakiness' is like.

Some top Côte d'Or producers still put their best Chardonnays into oak for a while, but they tend to keep the oak flavour more restrained and in harmony with the fruit. This is the ideal to which producers of Chardonnay all over the world aspire; some of them show every sign of beating the Burgundians at their own game. 'Just a kiss of oak' is what some California producers are trying to give their precious, wildly fashionable Chardonnays. By looking carefully at the wide range of different styles of Chardonnay available today, you should get a good idea of the extra richness in colour, body and flavour that oak gives to a white wine. You will also have reinforced the lessons already learnt about the influence of climate on wine.

a few really contrary treasures – Chardonnays from newish wine regions that taste confusingly like the lightly oaked aristocrats of the Côte d'Or. Hicks & Hayes of Maidenhead may still have some Tisdall Mount Helen Chardonnay from Australia; La Vigneronne and Adnams of Southwold may stock the wonderful Chalone Chardonnay of California, and the latter might even have some Stony Hill stashed away. Oak is doing its job properly when it's barely detectable.

Sémillon – a great rotter

Sémillon is a curiously obscure grape. Even members of the dwindling ranks of Sauternes lovers are often unaware of the crucial role played by the varietal in its production. No serious wine drinker would ever confess ignorance of or aversion to Chardonnay, but such is the Cinderella-like state in which the grape languishes that the word Sémillon is hardly ever found on a wine label.

Only in Australia, and especially in the Hunter Valley, is Semillon (l's pronounced and no accent) taken seriously as a varietal, to be vinified by itself as a dry white worthy of ageing and labelling as Semillon (though, just to be cussed about it, they sometimes call it Riesling – crazy). Youthful Australian Semillons provide a rare opportunity to taste the grape unblended with its habitual Bordeaux partner Sauvignon. We have already seen examples of dry white Graves, such as Domaine de Chevalier, made mainly from Sauvignon supplemented by the richness of Sémillon. Just down the road in Sauternes, Barsac and Bordeaux's less famous sweet wine districts, a bit of Sauvignon is often added to Sémillon to give the resultant blend a bit of extra acidity while keeping it predominantly Sémillon and sweet.

To see what the grape itself tastes like, try to track down a youthful Semillon from Australia or even one from California, where the grape is still quite widely cultivated. Notice, even on a fairly young example, a low acidity and yellowish colour, with hints of the spiciness to come. Roll it round the mouth to feel the full weight of the wine. You might even note a certain creamy texture with the smoothness of lanolin. Sémillon, like Chardonnay, is not seeringly aromatic and, with its relatively heavy body, it lumbers towards you rather than attacking you with a point of sharp flavour.

Sémillon is relatively low in acid, even weightier and more alcoholic than Chardonnay, and hence carries with it the suggestion of sweetness even when it is vinified dry. Some tasters find figs in its flavours, others cigars. It can sometimes have a slight edge of citrus and there's something almost waxy in its texture. Clues to the grape's identity are: a deep golden colour, lots of alcohol and low acidity.

You will be expected to make do with a fairly small sample of wine

As it ages it takes on an almost orange colour, whether it's a dry or sweet wine, and the mature dry Semillons of the Hunter Valley are some of the wine world's most curious and under-appreciated treasures. They are, it must be said, an acquired taste. The wines seem to lose their early message of the grape and take on the character of the land itself. Any Hunter wine more than a decade old starts to display a curious minerally taste which I call a 'volcanic twang' (to hoots of laughter from Australians, of course). This applies to every varietal cultivated there, and is the most striking example I have come across to support the traditional European view that the actual composition of the soil and subsoil in any region determines the flavour of wine produced there. (Californians argue that it is important only that the land is well drained to encourage deep roots seeking moisture and therefore a complex root system.) There is a high proportion of volcanic soil in the best bit of the Hunter, just as there is in Madeira – this may account for my 'twang'.

Try to get hold of an old Hunter Valley Semillon. As I write, they're thin on the ground in Britain, although Les Amis du Vin again have a Rothbury 1976 and Averys of Bristol, who were early pioneers of wines from Australia, might have a bottle or two lurking in their cellars. (I also have a hunch that Australian wines will be increasingly easy to find as producers there at last get interested in export markets.) Notice – in fact you won't be able to avoid it – the curiousness of the old Semillon's flavour, as well as its deep colour and weight. That is my volcanic twang: a taste almost of burnt earth, with lots of little mineral trace elements close to the surface. There's something reminiscent of those black charcoal biscuits served in gentlemen's clubs.

To experience Sémillon's greatest contribution to wine pleasure it is necessary to look at sweet white Bordeaux, especially the best wines from the communes of Sauternes and Barsac. (The first encompasses the second so that all Barsac is Sauternes but not all Sauternes is Barsac.) To make a great sweet wine you have to have grapes that contain an awful lot of sugar, so that even when you have fermented enough to produce the wine's alcohol content you are still left with lots of fruity richness.

You will get the most out of this tasting exercise if you arm yourself with two bottles (or, preferably, the infuriatingly elusive half-bottle size) of good quality Sauternes, one made in a botrytis-struck vintage and one from a growth in which botrytis was not encouraged to make its somewhat frightening appearance. (It makes the grapes look as though they're covered with thick grey cobwebby dust.) Good vintages for botrytis in recent years have been 1980, 1979 and 1975. Vintages in which good sweet white Bordeaux was made without the help of botrytis were 1981, 1978 and 1976. Find an example of a 'cru classé'

The best sweet white wines in the world share a common helper towards this gloriously luscious state, in a rather unsavoury-looking mould. In certain warm, moist autumns, this attacks the grapes and – without breaking them and causing spoilage – shrivels them to concentrate their sugar content. *Botrytis cinerea*, also known as noble rot, *pourriture noble* and *Edelfäule*, gives a special honeyed vegetal quality to the taste of overripe grapes. It occurs only in vintages when conditions are just right, and only in certain places. For years California's vine growers did their best to eliminate it because they didn't realize what lovely things it could do for grapes such as Riesling, Gewürztraminer, and Sémillon. Vintages that are too dry can produce sweet wines, but they won't have the curious whiff of *botrytis* – to which Sémillon, with its thin skin, is conveniently prone.

A-level: You could at this stage see whether you can detect the difference in taste between a sweet white Bordeaux that has been given some oak maturation and one that has been fermented and aged in the vat. Most of the *cru classé* châteaux of Sauternes still use oak. Indeed, they sometimes use it for too long, but less famous sweet wines from that region and most of those from the 'lesser' neighbours, such as Ste Croix du Mont and Loupiac, are no great friends of wood. Château Doisy-Daëne is an unusual example of a classed growth Sauternes in which the influence of wood is minimal.

château of Sauternes in each group, if you can afford it, but a less well known name for about £4 a bottle may well illustrate the point. Notice how the non-botrytis wines are very fruity and honeyed, but how the 'botrytized' wines seem if anything even sweeter, with an overlay in some of something that reminds me of slightly rotten cabbage and in others of luscious, unctuous spice. Mackie's of London EC4 make a speciality of Sauternes.

Botrytis strikes

Try out the oak-versus-inert-material-ageing exercise using different Chardonnays. If you take an inexpensive sweet white Bordeaux, say a Ste Croix du Mont, Loupiac or simply a basic Sauternes or Barsac with no château name on the label (most off-licence chains can offer what's called a 'generic' i.e. common or garden, Sauternes), you will notice the sweet unctuousness of the Sémillon grape. There will not, however, be any of the extra layers of flavour, such as of botrytis or of oak ageing, which underlines the intensity of a superior 'cru classé' château-bottled wine from Sauternes. Notice the deeper, browner colour in the superior wine.

Or, to reduce the variables even more, compare a Château Doisy-Daëne with a wine from the same vintage and from a property that is of equal standing but keener on oak maturation, such as Château Coutet, Climens, Suduiraut or Rieussec.

When a Riesling's not a Riesling

A simple qualitative exercise is long overdue, one which is particularly apt to illustrate the strange case of the non-Riesling Riesling. Probably the first wine of which I was conscious was served to my grandmother and me at a sedate Somerset luncheon party, and we called it Lutomer Rize-ling. We were wrong on two counts. We should have pronounced it *reece*-ling of course and, furthermore, the wine wasn't 'proper' Riesling at all, but from an unrelated and much less aristocratic grape that goes by names such as Welsch Riesling, Italian Riesling, Olasz Riesling and Laski Riesling. The only characteristic that this Welsch Riesling has in common with the noble Riesling of Germany – called Rhine Riesling, Rheinriesling, Rajinskirizling, White Riesling and Johannisberg Riesling outside Germany, – is that it is tends to make slightly perfumed, medium dry wines with a fair bit of acidity. The difference in quality should be apparent.

To prove to yourself what a good judge of wine you are, get hold of any German wine with the word Riesling on the label and one of the following: any Yugoslav Laski Riesling such as Lutomer, Cloberg or that from your local supermarket chain; or any Hungarian Olasz Riesling. Get someone to serve you a glass of each 'blind'. See how the racy acidity and pure, fresh perfume of one leaps out of the glass to encourage you to have another sip. The lesser wine (often called Rizling) should seem rather dull, even mousey, compared with the real Riesling.

The Austrians have managed to make some extremely good wines from the Welsch Riesling, including even some very sweet ones that earn the designation Trockenbeerenauslesen. And in the north-east of Italy there are also some light, fragrant Italian Rieslings. However, the 'lesser' varietal is most popular in Yugoslavia, Hungary and Romania, where it is encouraged to produce

The lesser Riesling is not a very easy wine to distinguish 'blind' because it's not strong on memorable characteristics. Not one of the wine world's greats, this, but a good illustration of the fact that wine's quality does vary greatly.

lots of rather undistinguished wine. Yugoslavia's Lutomer and Cloberg and Hungary's Pecs all derive from Laski Riesling.

Real Rhine Riesling is a much more finicky vine. It ripens late, so the vine grower always runs a risk that the crop will be lost, and it produces relatively little wine per vine (though the Germans are good at coaxing as much as possible from it). The entire German wine scene is centred on Riesling. Ninety-five per cent of Germany's fine wine is made from this single grape variety which, like Chardonnay, has been planted all over the world by winemakers aspiring to the exciting race and breed of the prototypes. Riesling, again like Chardonnay, changes considerably with age, but even in its early life it is marked by very zesty acid and a delicate flowery-fruit aroma which shouts refreshment rather than lubrication. It's difficult to think of food that is particularly well matched to Riesling, though Graf Matuschka-Greiffenclau of Schloss Vollrads has been working hard to counter this view with a range of *trocken* and *halbtrocken* (dry and half-dry) Rieslings. The grape is usually vinified to retain at least some residual sugar and this leaves the wines fairly low in alcohol, hence their delicacy.

In the world of wine, as in every other, what we have least of is what we want most. The winemaker in southern Italy or California tries desperately to keep the acidity level in his wines up under the powerful glare of the ripening sun. His counterpart at the northern limit of German vine cultivation lusts after

Rhine Riesling ripens late so the grower always runs the risk that the crop will be lost

Now study, and try to memorize, the particular appeal of the real Riesling. Of course, the more you have spent on your German Riesling example, the stronger will be the Riesling characteristics and class. But even a fairly humble example should have the very appealing combination of high acidity (notice how the edges of your tongue start to crinkle in anticipation even as you smell the wine) with a lovely smell that suggests fresh Alpine flowers. (There's nothing too exotic and heady about the Riesling, unlike the Gewürztraminer.) The lightness of body is a good giveaway for a German Riesling, as is a certain amount of sweetness following the lovely fruity perfume. Try to imprint this palate picture on your memory, for the aroma of the Riesling grape should be one of the most distinctive of all. Honey-and-flowers is a common tasting note.

The French tend to call their wines after the place they come from; the 'appellation contrôlée' system of designating the better wines enshrines Meursault and Sancerre rather than Chardonnay and Sauvignon. Newer wine regions, such as California and Australia, major on grape variety or varietal. The more sunshine to ripen his grapes, and the most prized German wines are those highest in natural sugar. Only in the sunniest vintages is much sweet wine made there. But Riesling Beerenauslesen and Trockenbeeren-auslesen, picked very late to trap every last ray of sunshine in the bottle, can provide more good examples of *botrytis* or *Edelfäule* – at a price.

The French tend to name their wine after the place they came from

The very sweet Rieslings, *TBA*s and *BA*s, are usually fiendishly expensive. Curiously, however, wines that are only medium dry to medium sweet, *spätlesen* and *auslesen*, can often be good value – especially if they have a bit of age on them, as standard German pricing practice seems to have ignored inflation. Such wines can provide wonderful examples of what happens to Riesling as it ages. Just like

Germans also often specify the grape variety together with the place it was grown (e.g. Bereich Bernkastel Riesling), but their quality designation system revolves around the ripeness of the grapes when they were picked – and hence, usually, the sweetness of the resultant wine. This means that their most prized wines are called either Trockenbeeren-auslese or Beerenauslese. They're very sweet, very rare and very expensive. To examine the effects of unusual ripeness on the Riesling grape in Germany, look instead for one of the next two rungs down, Auslese and Spätlese. There is usually noticeable sweetness on the tip of the tongue in such wines, and yet the balancing high acidity will stop them from being remotely cloying. See if you can detect any of the vegetabley, cabbagey smell of botrytis as already experienced with Sémillon.

A-level: A good Sauternes and a 'TBA' or 'BA' are both extremely sweet and unctuous. They might also both have a whiff of botrytis about them. The way to distinguish between them is to look for the flowery fragrance of the Riesling grape, much more distinctive than the bouquet of rich Sémillon.

Try to find an example of a mature Riesling in order to be impressed by how wonderfully this grape ages. Although in its youth it appears so frail and appetizing, it seems to gain strength over the years and adds all sorts of flavours to the initial grape aroma. Among recent years in which Rieslings suitable for ageing were made in Germany are 1976, 1975 and 1971. Wines of, say, Spätlese quality and above from these mature Chardonnay and Sémillon, the wine takes on a more intense colour, often a deep gold but in this case with a greenish tinge, almost gamboge. The bouquet evolves into something much more layered than the simple floweriness of young Riesling. It is faintly reminiscent of petrol, though still enticing and extremely pure in its appeal. A Riesling is often steely but the fruity acidity is its most obvious distinguishing mark. As it ages, this acidity becomes more apparent while the sweetness seems to recede. When it is too old (either from a poorish vintage such as 1973, or because it has come to the end of what might be a very long run) the wine seems to taste dry and too tart.

vintages should by now be fairly deep golden-green in colour, still retain lots of acidity and have developed a much more complex nose. Notice that curious 'old Riesling' smell that I associate with petrol or something more agreeably oily, at least.

Note that the most basic qualities of German wines, called 'Kabinett' or (even more basic) 'QbA' or 'Qualitätswein', are designed for early drinking. Ordinary German wine should be drunk just as soon as you can. Hang on only to wines of Spätlese, Auslese, BA or TBA quality. And 99 per cent of all the lesser Welsch Riesling made should be drunk in its youth.

The effect of climate on taste is well illustrated even within the fairly close wine regions of Germany. German wine is sold either in green or brown bottles, the green ones coming from the Mosel and its tributaries, the Saar and Ruwer, and the brown from Rhine river regions such as the Rheingau, Rheinhessen and Rheinpfalz. Because they are even cooler than Rhine vineyards, those on the steep slopes of the Mosel produce lighter, crisper wines. Some of them may have only about 6° of alcohol, while those of the Rhine are at least one degree stronger and taste noticeably more substantial. Travelling upriver past the Rheingau to Rheinhessen (for Liebfraumilch) and Rheinpfalz, one encounters increasingly fuller-bodied wines that have gained intensity and ripeness with more sunshine.

A-level: It can be confusing trying to distinguish a Mosel Auslese, say,

Germany has eleven distinct wine regions, of which only the Mosel-Saar-Ruwer (one region), Rheingau, Rheinhessen and Rheinpfalz (or Palatinate) send much wine to Britain. The regions are listed in increasing order of sunniness and richness of wines produced. Try to get hold of an example of even ordinary 'QbA' wine from each region (though the Rheingau specializes in top-quality wines) and contrast the weight and style of the wines. Mosel wines, in the green bottles, are lightweight and 'slatey' sharp. Rheingau wines seem to have the most judicious balance of Riesling fruit and northerly acidity. Rheinhessen wines tend to be a bit flabby and a huge proportion of them end up as Liebfraumilch, while the Rheinpfalz, with the most sunshine of all and some interesting soils and grapes, turns out Germany's spiciest wines.

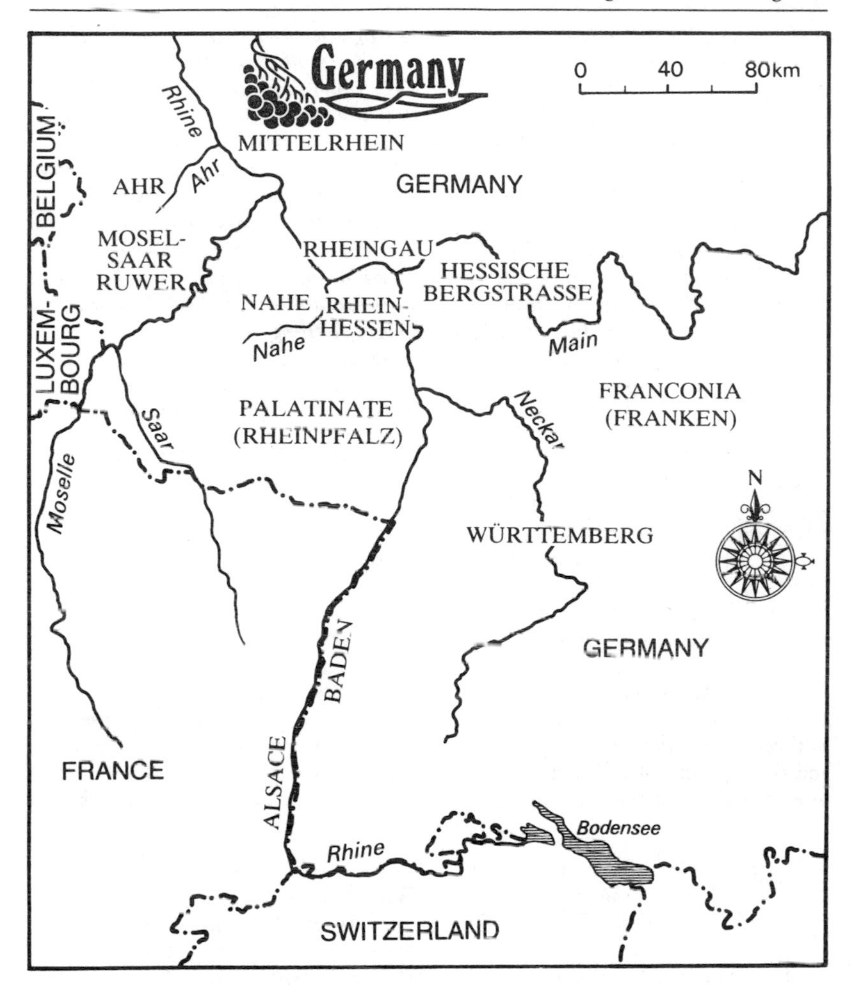

from a Rheingau Kabinett. The first will be relatively light in body but high in sugar, while the converse is true of the second.

Riesling is the most respected wine cultivated in Alsace just across the Rhine from Rheinpfalz, cheek by jowl with the rather richer Gewürztraminer grape. It should be

Try out an Alsace Riesling. Hugel wines are quite easy to find, but any producer will do. Notice how the wines have the same pure flowery Riesling smell and the suggestion of

easy to distinguish an Alsace Riesling (which in some ways gives a particularly clear picture of the aroma of the Riesling grape) from most German wines because Alsace winemakers ferment all the sugar out to make dry wines. They still have the perfumed floweriness on the nose, but are dry on the palate. Now, however, there is a vogue for dry wines in Germany and these *trocken* can sometimes be confused with Alsace wines, though they're usually lighter.

lots of refreshing acidity on the nose. When you test out the sweetness on your tongue, however, you will see that the Alsace wine is almost bone dry. It is certainly much drier than any German Riesling, other than one of the newfangled 'trocken' or 'halbtrocken' wines designed for the diet-conscious German market.

See if you can distinguish blind between an Alsace Riesling and a Mosel Riesling. The key is in the weight, or body, of each. Many Alsace wines are almost double the alcoholic strength of some Mosels.

The grape they call the Rhine Riesling has been very successful and popular in Australia, especially in the Eden Valley and Clare. Being from Southern Hemisphere vineyards harvested in February and March, such a vintage-dated wine always has a good six months' greater age than European equivalents. Moreover, Australian Rhine Rieslings seem to age very rapidly. Even after as little as three years, they are deep yellow and busy giving off all sorts of interesting petrol-like signs of age.

An Australian Rhine Riesling can provide an excellent, if rather accelerated, example of what happens to the grape with age. Few firms specialize in Australia, but Victoria Wine, W. H. Cullen and Averys should be able to provide a few examples. Look out for Orlando Rhine Rieslings which are representative specimens of the delicate touch possessed by some Australian winemakers. Australian Rieslings are characterized by a little bit of 'spritz' and not that much sugar.

California has also had unexpected success with the grape they call the Johannisberg or White Riesling. The wines have much more body and alcohol than their German counterparts, but careful winemakers have kept acidity levels well up. They can be very attractive, flowery medium dry wines that, like Beaujolais, are so obviously gulpable that they are strong candidates for that rather puzzling epithet 'real drinking wines'.

Les Amis du Vin of London W12, the Wine Studio, SW1, and La Vigneronne, SW7, are good sources for California Johannisberg or White Rieslings (same thing). Joseph Phelps have a German winemaker who makes lovely wines from the grape he grew up with. Most California examples are well balanced even though much fuller bodied than German wines. Note the flowery Riesling smell overlaid with extra west-coast ripeness. Many of California's Rieslings seem to me to have the rather exotic edge of lime on a honeyed Riesling flavour.

German commoners

Germany also produces a wide range of wines from grapes less aristocratic than the Riesling. Most of them are modelled on it, some exaggerating its aromatic qualities to the point of obviousness, others being too pale a shadow. They tend to be cheaper than Rieslings, so it pays to develop a taste for what they have to offer.

Müller-Thurgau is Germany's most widely planted grape variety, a century-old crossing inspired by Riesling but without such refreshingly high acidity and with a much softer, grapier aroma. The crossing was developed to be a much less risky, earlier-ripening grape than the Riesling, and this is translated into a much less interesting range of flavours in the resulting wine. Its advantage is that it has a high yield and can flourish in spots where Riesling can't, but

don't expect greatness from it and drink it young. For much the same reasons as in Germany, the Müller-Thurgau is popular with grape growers in England and in that other wine region far from the Equator, New Zealand, where they rather naughtily call it Riesling Sylvaner.

Because Müller-Thurgau has no great cachet in Germany, not too many labels specify it. Most Liebfraumilch is substantially made up of Müller-Thurgau, however, even though it may be tarted up a bit with something like Morio-Muskat (see below). Well over a quarter of Germany's vineyards are planted with this grape variety.

Perhaps the easiest way to taste unadorned Müller-Thurgau is to find an English example. Lamberhurst Priory in Kent make a very attractive one, as they do nearby at Spots Farm. English wines are, in the main, made from Germanic grapes and tend to taste like German wines, only much drier. This means that there are strong similarities between English wines and Germany's new 'trocken' and 'halbtrocken' wines. The Vintner's Wain, in Buckingham Palace Road, is a good place to buy British as is the English Wine Centre of Alfriston.

New Zealand winemakers often manage to make from the Müller-Thurgau something a little more vibrant than their Northern Hemisphere counterparts. Try Peter Dominic, Victoria Wine, Waitrose, Gough Bros and W. H. Cullen for examples of their light, fruity and often slightly 'spritz' style.

Sylvaner is a straightforward grape grown extensively in Germany and Alsace which has pronounced acidity and usually not much else.

Look for character in an Alsace Sylvaner and notice how difficult it can be to find it. Trimbach can sometimes make an example that's so racy it is just like a Riesling, but most others are simple crisp dry wines with just a faint whiff of Alsace pungency.

German grape breeders have more recently been at work on varieties with even more obviously aromatic appeal – partly because they are useful for converting duller base wine into something that tastes faintly Riesling-like. (It is well known that lots of very ordinary Italian wine is 'Germanized' in this way.) Morio-Muskat is one of the most aromatic grape variety crossings, and has strong Muscat, i.e. grapey, characteristics. Many inexpensive German *QbA* and *Tafelwein* bottles (the lowest quality level) contain a bit of Morio-Muskat. Very scented cachous.

You will almost certainly have drunk some Morio-Muskat, if only as a small part of a cheap German blend. Victoria Wine and Asda sell a perfectly creditable, very spicy medium-dry litre from the Rheinpfalz.

Scheurebe is one of the most promising new crossings. When the grape is ripe it can make very fine dessert wines with some of the elegance of Riesling. When it doesn't ripen fully, however, it can be quite unpleasantly catty.

We will probably see more and more wines labelled Scheurebe. Watch out for examples in the Spätlese category and above, and look for a certain blackcurrant-leaf flavour.

Chenin Blanc and a bit of cloning

Chenin Blanc is unusual in that it is grown extensively throughout the world's wine regions, with enormous variation in the taste of the wine it produces. It makes fairly ordinary wines in the main, but is clearly capable of greatness.

The home of the Chenin Blanc is the Loire Valley and, in particular, the long middle stretch upriver from Muscadet country towards the distant vineyards of Sancerre and Pouilly Fumé. It is the basic grape of Anjou Blanc, Saumur (still and sparkling) and Vouvray (still, sparkling, sweet and dry). Even within the confines of the tiny appellation Vouvray, the versatility of the grape is demonstrated. There it makes wines of all degrees of sweetness, fizziness and potential. Basic Loire Chenin Blanc has a faint honey-and-flowers smell, not totally unlike Riesling but with less distinction and more body. Like any Loire wine, these basic Chenins have lots and lots of acidity – remember the Sauvignon exercise with latitude?

To experience plain, unadorned Loire Chenin Blanc, try any white wine labelled Anjou, Saumur or Vouvray. Notice the fruity, appetizing nature of the wine. There is lots of acidity and some honeyed, almost peachy flavour but noticeably more body and 'breadth' than the Riesling grape would give. Most off-licences can offer an everyday example of one of these wines, and Yapp Bros of Mere, Wilts., specialize in examples with lots of character. 'Damp straw' is my trigger expression.

There are little pockets of vineyards on the Loire, however, where the Chenin Blanc can produce honeyed wines that can last, if not for ever, certainly for half as long. When they're young, they have so much acidity that it is difficult to believe they have much sweetness in them at all. But, as they mature, they develop a lovely, round, almost 'gummy' character that takes them closer to the golden syrup mould. Wines such as Vouvray and Montlouis are usually made in a wide range of degrees of richness, from *sec*, through *demi-sec* to *moelleux*. After a decade or two the colour takes on a wonderful golden lustre; but the key to a Loire Chenin Blanc, however old and however sweet, is very high acidity together with some honey and a suggestion of summer flowers.

Palpably better quality, and often ludicrously underpriced, are the wines of Savennières, Quarts de Chaume, Bonnezeaux and those of quality-conscious Vouvray producers such as Gaston Huet, A. Foreau, Marc Brédif and Daniel Jarry. Try Yapp again, O. W. Loeb of London SW1 and Ferrers le Mesurier of Northants. These are wines with real honey (especially if, as in some Bonnezeaux, Quarts de Chaume and Vouvray in 1976, botrytis has struck) and a gold colour. Acidity will always be high but the richness of the wines gradually builds up. There is a superior Anjou, Moulin Touchais, whose 1959 appears to be ubiquitous (try any 'proper' wine merchant) and to be a good fifteen years younger than the date on the label. I have never tasted a Loire wine of this type that seemed over the hill – and I have

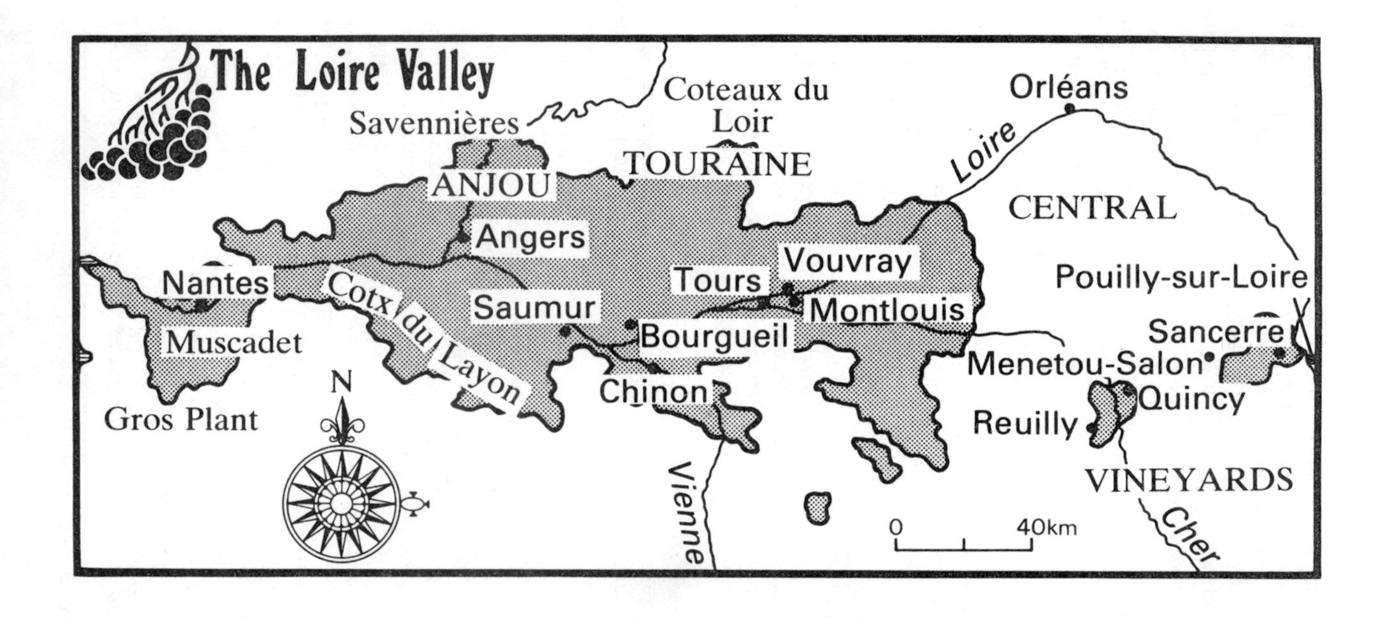
The Loire Valley
Savennières
Coteaux du
Loir
Orléans
Loire
TOURAINE
ANJOU
CENTRAL
Angers
Vouvray
Nantes
Tours
Pouilly-sur-Loire
Cotx du Layon
Saumur
Montlouis
Sancerre
Muscadet
Bourgueil
Menetou-Salon
Chinon
Quincy
N
Gros Plant
Reuilly
Vienne
VINEYARDS
0
40km
Cher

Chenin Blanc is grown widely in California, Australia, South Africa (where it is very popular and usually called Steen) and South America. What is puzzling is how unlike Loire Chenins these wines taste. Standard California Chenin Blanc is pretty neutral, used for straightforward medium dry inexpensive wines that provide a good base for the winemaker's skill. South African Steens are different again, with a bit more race, character (and *spritz*) to them. They're often firm and pleasant, but not reminiscent of either the Loire or California. The explanation for these wide variations may lurk in that science-fiction word 'clone'. A single cutting of a vine type can be responsible for the future of that varietal in a new wine region. The Australian wine industry owes its existence to a handful of vine cuttings taken out there by the first settlers, for instance. It is possible that the Chenin Blanc of California and the Steen of South Africa stem from clones of the varietal that emphasize characteristics rather different both from each other and from the original Chenin Blanc of the Loire. Just a slight variance from the original plants could well have become exaggerated over the years. Clonal selection, choosing a particular plant because it has the characteristics one wants, plays an increasing role in the world of wine. Germany leads in this technique of making sure you have the sort of vines you want by planting only selected clones of them. You can choose plants for a high yield, high quality and resistance to all sorts of pests, diseases and conditions.

tasted several wines from the 1920s.

A California Chenin Blanc should not be too difficult to find (The Wine Studio of London SW1 specialize in California). It will probably be a soft medium dry wine with none of the bite and 'wet straw' of the Loire example. Collisons of London SW1 or the Cape Wine Centres of W1 and Edinburgh will have a score of South African Steens (they are surprisingly widely stocked, especially the KWV Chenin Blanc). Notice the appetizing, slightly 'spritzy' quality of these wines. Their positive, almost smoky character to me can be more reminiscent of a slightly sweet, very youthful basic Mâcon (Chardonnay) than an Anjou (Chenin Blanc from the Loire). Try to taste at least two of these three possibilities together so as to get an accurate idea of the contrasts between them. Look out for Chenin Blancs from other parts of the world and see how they shape up to the Loire model.

4 The raw material – red grapes

How to make wine red

The principles of making a white wine were outlined on page 76. If you followed those steps with a black grape you would end up, amazingly enough, with a wine that was white – possibly very pale pink. The flesh of all but a handful of obscure grape varieties is the same colour: sludge green. Colouring materials, pigments, can be found only in the skin of the grape.

Take a black grape and peel it. Do the same to a white grape and notice that they are almost indistinguishable.

This means that to make a red wine, or rather to make a wine red, it is essential to keep the grape skins in contact with the must so that the pigments will be attracted out of the skins and into the resultant wine. Conveniently, the heat generated by the fermentation process puts everything into a stewing state, and this hastens along the colour-extraction process. Otherwise fermentation happens just as with white wines.

As further evidence of how a white wine can be made from black grapes by carefully running the juice off the skins before fermentation, you need only consider Champagne (better still – drink some). Well over half the Champagne vineyards are planted with the black-skinned Pinot grapes. The Californians also made lots of wines called Blanc de Noirs when they had vineyards full of black grapes, and there was a fashion for white wines. Some of these wines were made by careful separation of skins and must, others by charcoal 'bleaching' of the wines (just as is done to make Pale Cream Sherries).

On page 40 we examined some of the factors governing how much colour a wine has. Some grapes are higher in natural pigments than others, as we shall see below. Grenache is a pale grape, as are some clones of Pinot Noir, while Cabernet Sauvignon and Syrah are very thick skinned and therefore great potential donors of colouring matter to the must. Some years encourage thicker

Notice how pale the Grenache-based reds of Lirac and Tavel can be, as can many red Burgundies. Claret (Cabernet Sauvignon) and Hermitage (Syrah) tend to be very deeply coloured, however. We shall be considering this in more detail. Look out for the colour of different vintages of Bordeaux, another subject to be studied in more depth later.

skins than others. The weather preceding the Bordeaux vintages 1980, 1977 and 1974 was wet, and diluted the colour as well as the quality of the Clarets of those years.

By leaving the skins in contact with the must for a protracted period, the winemaker can give extra colour to the resultant wine. However, he has to be careful not to overdo it, as bitter tannic elements will seep out at the same time as the pigments. The must may be left 'on the skins', as they say, for anything from a few days to three weeks. Extra colour and tannin can be obtained by pressing the leftover skins and adding that 'press wine' to the original wine that was pumped from or run out of the fermentation vat.

One of the hallmarks of top quality Claret, a classed growth wine (one that says 'cru classé' on the label and was included in the 1855 classification of the Médoc and Graves), is that the wine has been given a fairly long 'cuvaison', time for the must to macerate on the skins. Compare the colour of a wine such as this with one from the same vintage but from an ordinary property, a 'petit château' that is not 'classé', or a blending vat.

Another means of making red wine and extracting a lot of colour out of the grapes quickly is carbonic maceration or 'whole grape fermentation'. Beaujolais is made by a version of this technique, which involves fermenting the grapes without breaking them. The heat builds up inside them and by the action of carbon dioxide in the absence of oxygen another sort of alcoholic fermentation happens naturally. This makes very supple fruity wines that are not designed for a long life, because they don't contain lots of tannin, but are very deeply coloured. (The grapes at the bottom of the vat are crushed, which means they ferment in the traditional way.)

To examine the fruity charm and deep colour given by carbonic maceration and allied techniques, arm yourself with a Beaujolais, a Côtes-du-Rhône, and a Claret such as Sichel's Belair or one from the innovative winemaker Pierre Coste (whose wines are stocked by Adnams of Southwold). What all these very different wines have in common is a very low-tannin, supple attraction in which the fruity character is emphasized, and there to be enjoyed only months after the vintage.

Gamay the gulpable

Gamay, the grape responsible for Beaujolais, is for most tasters the

It's sad but true that to experience the real taste of Gamay at its best

easiest varietal to recognize in a red wine. Even the colour is distinctive: crimson with a definite purplish tinge, making Beaujolais one of the 'bluest' wines in the world. The smell is even more tell-tale though, and even more difficult to describe than that of other grapes. Gamay is always high in refreshing acidity (these wines are really 'white' in function if not in hue) and just one whiff will have your tongue crinkling. Then there's a smell that I describe as 'juicyfruit', sometimes with a slightly inky edge. The standard tasting note on Beaujolais is always 'fresh and fruity', the freshness being that acidity, and the fruitiness the very simple but undeniable appeal of the Gamay grape. You know when you smell it that it's not a great wine, but it's so eminently gulpable that any genuine well-made example will woo you into the glass.

you should avoid British-bottled Beaujolais. Some bottlers over here manage to retain the essential freshness, but too many somehow let it escape as they rumble the wine across the Channel in tankers. To form your impression of Gamay look for Beaujolais that has been bottled in the region. Straightforward Piat de Beaujolais, easy to find, would give you the flavour. So should any wine from Georges Duboeuf (available from Davisons and Gough Bros), Loron, Dépagneux and from the only Beaujolais specialist in this country, Roger Harris of Weston Longville in Norfolk. Notice the colour and distinctive smell, definitely an aroma and not a bouquet (see Glossary). One good example should be enough to imprint that Gamay character on your memory.

Gamay usually produces fairly lightweight wines but you may come across examples that seem medium or even full bodied. In many cases this will be because of a mechanical-sounding winemaking technique called chaptalization, the adding of sugar to the grape must (*not* to the wine) and then fermenting it out so as to make the resultant wine stronger. This is perfectly legal in France and, if carefully done, does nothing to the flavour of the wine, but simply adds body. It is usually beet sugar that is added though there are moves within the EEC to turn some of its wine lake into concentrated grape must that could be used instead.

Remember that a light-bodied red wine, such as the sort of Beaujolais the Gamay produces unaided by over-chaptalization, can take a certain amount of chilling if you want a drink for refreshment. In any case the Gamay is not a grape that gives off so many fascinating nuances of flavour that you need to encourage this vaporization by warmth. Standard practice in the region itself is to serve Beaujolais 'cellar cool', at about 52°F. Beaujolais is the perfect wine in circumstances in which you can't govern serving temperature too strictly, such as on a picnic. It can bear a wide range of temperatures, so if you chilled it before setting off you would probably still enjoy it at the much warmer temperature it reached by the end of your picnic.

Gamay-based wines are very rarely suitable for ageing. Their chief purpose is to refresh and give gulping pleasure while still youthful – sometimes still in the nursery, like all that Beaujolais Nouveau. A *cru* Beaujolais, from one of the nine special villages, can gain depth and interest for about five years after the good vintage, and the wines from Moulin-à-Vent can age into an almost Burgundian state of maturity.

Look for the following names on the label to enjoy superior Beaujolais from these 'crus': Fleurie, Chiroubles, St Amour, Chénas, Juliénas, Brouilly, Côte de Brouilly, Morgon, Moulin-à-Vent. A wine labelled Beaujolais-Villages will usually taste a little firmer and juicier than a straight Beaujolais, while these 'cru' wines have positive character of their own.

Other Gamay-based French wines are usually called Gamay on the label (Beaujolais very rarely is) and are made in Touraine on the Loire, in the Ardèche and the Côtes d'Auvergne, du Forez and Roannaises. However, these are rarely as interesting and lively as Beaujolais. The grape is also responsible for light reds in Austria and Hungary, and a strange rather sweet variation of it can be found in California labelled as Napa Gamay – but not Gamay Beaujolais, which is a clone of the Burgundy grape Pinot Noir. Most confusing, and neither of them is as good as Beaujolais.

Victoria Wine, bless 'em, list a Gamay for inexpensive sampling from the Loire's cleverly named Jardin de la France, and many Gamays de Touraine can also be found cheaply. French non-Beaujolais Gamays tend to be a little austere. Many Austrian reds contain Blaufränkisch, and 'Kekfrancos' is grown on the Austro-Hungarian border near Sopron. It also goes into Bull's Blood. These and the California 'Gamays' can be not austere enough.

Around the world with Cabernet Sauvignon

Cabernet Sauvignon is the grape variety before which lovers of fine wine should genuflect. Pinot Noir may be responsible for a few thousand bottles of great red Burgundy every year, but the Cabernet Sauvignon is the main ingredient in millions of bottles of wine with enormous ageing potential made all over the world. It has the winning combination of producing top quality wine and adapting well

to a wide range of climates and soils, while retaining its basic character.

Not to put too chauvinistic a point on it, it's rather like the English language. From its home base Bordeaux (which at one time was ruled by the English crown) it can now be found in a similar form but with different accents throughout the globe – particularly in America, South Africa, Australia and New Zealand. With the emphasis on 'varietal labelling' in these newer wine regions, it is very easy to pick out wines made from this – the greatest – red grape variety. In its homeland Bordeaux, however, less than one per cent of all the wine made from it will actually specify Cabernet Sauvignon on the label. This is partly because red Bordeaux (or Claret, as we British call it, after the light *clairet* we used to ship from western France in the Middle Ages) is made from a mixture that consists mainly of Cabernet together with some other grapes. The other factor is the French *appellation contrôlée* system's concentration on geography. If you see any of the words listed opposite on the label, then the predominant grape variety in a red wine is almost certain to be Cabernet Sauvignon.

Bear in mind that, contrary to popular opinion, the Cabernet Sauvignon is not the most widely planted variety in Bordeaux. Most red wines carrying the general *appellation* Bordeaux will be made in the Cabernet Sauvignon style, even though they may contain a high proportion of other Bordeaux grapes, its less emphatic country cousin Cabernet Franc (see below),

To form an impression of what Cabernet Sauvignon tastes like when reared in its original Bordelais setting, look for a bottle of Claret, as fine as you can afford. The standard Claret bottle, with straight sides and a narrow neck, is easy to recognize and it often even has a label proclaiming a château name. The key to likely quality is the 'appellation' specified on the label. 'Bordeaux' is the most basic 'appellation' and might not present a very distinctive model for your palate picture of Cabernet Sauvignon. 'Bordeaux Supérieur' is the same quality level and merely means that the wine is slightly more alcoholic, say 11° as opposed to 10.5°. Most really good Claret carries a more specific 'appellation'. Try to find one from some territory that is respected as a producer of the finest Cabernet Sauvignon in the world: St Estèphe, Pauillac, St Julien, Margaux, Haut-Médoc, Médoc or Graves. Specific châteaux whose vineyards are planted with a high proportion of Cabernet Sauvignon, and whose wines are therefore very good examples of the varietal's characteristics, include (you should be so rich) Mouton-Rothschild, Grand Puy Lacoste, Branaire Ducru and Brane-Cantenac. Cabernet should, however, dominate in the blend of any wine with the 'appellations' specified above.

Notice in your sample of fine Bordeaux Cabernet the intensity of everything; colour, flavour and length are all very pronounced. The only ingredient in which Claret is relatively short is alcohol. Smell the

Bordeaux
0
20km
N
GIRONDE
MÉDOC
St Estèphe
Pauillac
St. Julien
BLAYAIS
HAUT-MÉDOC
BORDEAUX APPELLATION
BOURG
BORDEAUX APPELLATION
Margaux
FRONSAC
POMEROL
SAINT EMILION
Vayres
Bordeaux
PREMIERES CÔTES
ENTRE-DEUX-MERS
SAINTE-FOY
GRAVES
Cérons
Loupiac
SAUTERNES
Barsac
Ste Croix-du-Mont
BORDEAUX APPELLATION
Garonne

the Merlot of St Emilion and Pomerol in the north-east of the region, or the less distinguished Malbec grown on the Bordeaux fringes.

The Cabernet grape itself is small and blue, grows tightly clustered and, when pressed and fermented, usually has lots of tannin and colour to give to the must. The keynotes of youthful Cabernet are a very deep purple ink colour, the aroma of blackcurrants (not totally unlike the related Sauvignon Blanc) and, usually, lots of acidity and tannin. Claret, unlike some hot-country Cabernets, is only light to medium bodied, but its flavour is very intense and there is often a very lingering finish. A good Cabernet is capable of ageing superbly and many, with their high level of tannin, demand it.

wine and try to register that blackcurrant flavour. This grape aroma may be overlaid with the flavour of oak, something we shall examine in more detail, if the wine has been given pronounced wood ageing. For the pure grape aroma, try a Pierre Coste Graves from Adnams of Southwold or Lay & Wheeler of Colchester. He produces good examples of Bordeaux Cabernet without any oak influence. *See page 120 for more on oak.*

To get a suitably well informed impression of Cabernet, you should probably force yourself to sample the huge range of wines made from the grape around the world. Outside Bordeaux, but still in France, surprisingly little Cabernet is grown – only in the outlying regions, such as Bergerac and Côtes de Buzet, and in tiny pockets planted by the quality-conscious, as at Château Vignelaure in Provence. Further afield there are delicious Cabernets made in California, Washington State, Argentina and – especially delicious – Chile (though much of the Cabernet there may be the lesser Cabernet Franc, according to Miguel Torres, winemaker extraordinaire of Catalonia and Chile). New Zealand and Australia have substantial Cabernet plantings, with Coonawarra Cabernets winning greatest acclaim. South African specimens are beefy but definitely Cabernet, and there are plantings in Lebanon (Château Musar), Greece (Château Carras), Bulgaria (cheap and now available as part of the Hirondelle range), Yugoslavia (variable), Italy (soft and good value in the north-east and a great asset for noble wines in Tuscany) and

Spain (in Catalonia, to best effect in Torres Gran Coronas). Try to extract the Cabernet character from each of these wines whenever you have the chance to taste them. Probably the cheapest way to experience Cabernet fruit is in one of the less expensive California varietals. But there is a very alcoholic snag, as detailed in the next section.

Cabernet and climate

Because Cabernet Sauvignon is grown in so many different settings it is very useful as an illustration of the effect of the climate of an area on the style of wines produced there. The Cabernets of Bordeaux, in a temperate climate on the fairly chilly Atlantic seaboard, display the quintessence of the variety with lots of fruit, but they are low in alcohol and have marked acidity. Cabernets produced in New Zealand, with a climate at least as cold, are even lighter in body and are also often drier and more acid. Washington State Cabernets and some of those produced in the cooler parts of north-east Italy represent the slightly fuller, fruitier style of Cabernet that results from, among other things, rather hotter summers than are usual in Bordeaux and New Zealand.

Your first example of Claret, as suggested in the previous exercise, will do admirably to demonstrate Cabernet from a temperate climate. Notice that you find it really rather appetizing. Another glass with food would be pretty nice, though the high level of tannin in youthful Claret means that it's difficult to drink without food, and seems even tougher if served too cool. Claret has been described as the ultimate beverage wine. Almost any wine merchant or licensed outlet should be able to offer Clarets by the score. Traditional City and St James's Street merchants make a speciality of it. New Zealand Cabernets such as Cook's or Montana are so light and dry they can be almost weedy, and you may have to hunt the flavour. Victoria Wine and La Vigneronne of London SW7 are the places most likely to stock the obscure wines of NZ and Washington State.

To see the most dramatic examples of the impact of unmitigated sunshine on a red grape variety in general, and on Cabernet Sauvignon in particular, it is necessary to look at one of California's heavyweights.

Very few California Cabernets will not prove the point about the difference a hottish climate makes to the richness of the wine made there. Choose your example by the alcohol content on the label. Cabernets of

Full-bodied, ripe-to-the-point-of-plumminess Cabernets are not difficult to find there; indeed, it takes a great deal of ingenuity to produce a California Cabernet that is not too high in alcohol, and everything else too. Look at the depth of colour in these (often inexpensive) wines. When you look down into it, you will probably find it difficult to locate the bottom of the glass through the wine. The smell will be so strong, it'll have blackcurrant and practically every other fruit you can imagine. Many sought-after Napa Cabernets even have a hint of mint or eucalyptus overlaid on all this. In fact, a certain mintiness is a good giveaway to a California Cabernet. A feeling of faintheartedness in the taster when offered a second glass is another indication that here is a wine made from grape ripened to a merciless level of potential alcohol by the relentless Californian sunshine.

14° are by no means uncommon in California. You will notice, as well as the viscosity and the burn in the finish of such a high-alcohol wine, much less acidity than in your Bordeaux example and a richness that tastes almost sweet. Watch out for the distinctive minty, eucalyptus flavour in some more expensive California Cabs, made famous by Heitz Martha's Vineyard. Some California Cabernets can, however, be confused with some Clarets. A youthful, very concentrated Claret from a ripe year that is high in extract because it has had a long 'cuvaison' can seem very like the deep-coloured, intense wines of California – especially since top producers in California use exactly the same sort of barrels as the Bordelais (sometimes even from the same cooper). Look for the lower alcohol level, as a good indication that the wine was made on this side of the Atlantic.

Other examples of hot-country Cabernets, with concomitant effects on colour and alcohol levels, are Château Musar (though Cabernet is here blended with Rhône grapes) and many Australian and South African 'Cabs'. A common sight in wines from these two countries, both of whose reds often taste very hot, is a blackish tinge – almost as though the flavour has been steamed out of them. Although I rarely aspire to pinpointing the exact region in each country, I can usually tell a South African Cabernet from an Australian because the former is sweet and chocolatey, while the latter has a more minerally whiff about it.

The Château Musar wines show great spicy character with surprising finesse. Try the 1970 if you ever get the chance; Les Amis du Vin stock it. Coonawarra is one of Australia's most established areas for Cabernet, and Victoria Wine list Wynn's. Try Collison's for Cape Cabernets, of which Meerlust's blend Rubicon with classic Bordeaux grapes is the best I've tasted.

The other Cabernet

Although 'blending' is seen as a dirty word by so many wine drinkers, the most famous wine in the world, Claret, is very much a blended wine. Almost all Bordeaux estates, usually called Château Quelquechose, are planted with a mixture of grapes. Even those such as the top Médoc and Graves wines, which are predominantly Cabernet Sauvignon, will have a bit of something else planted alongside and blended into the final wine.

Here is a grape ripened under the relentless Californian sun

The most common 'other grape' is Cabernet Franc. It is often rather contemptuously dismissed as a lesser version of the Cabernet Sauvignon, but it can't be all that bad. Château Cheval Blanc, the top property of St Emilion whose wines sell at the same price as Château Lafite-Rothschild, is made up of two thirds Cabernet Franc. Cabernet Franc is known as Bouchet in St Emilion and nearby Pomerol, the two communes that complement Médoc and Graves on the other side of the Gironde to make up Bordeaux's top red wine area. (Cabernet Sauvignon ripens later than Cabernet Franc and can't ripen well in St Emilion/Pomerol.)

Cabernet Franc tastes similar to Cabernet Sauvignon, but is usually even more herbaceous, almost weedy. And because the grapes themselves are bigger, the wines are less tannic and are lighter coloured. The grape is planted extensively in the middle Loire and in northern Italy, where it produces luscious fruity wines with an edge of acidity

For pure, unblended Cabernet Franc try to taste a red Loire such as Chinon, Bourgueil, or slightly more intense and long lived, St Nicolas de Bourgueil. There's a certain juiciness, though it's less fruity than Beaujolais. My trigger word is 'pencil shavings' for the distinctive aroma of these wines – and I mean the wood bit rather than the lead. I hope you can and grassiness. They are rarely designed for a long life, however, and most Cabernet Franc wines are simple and gulpable, in the style of Beaujolais. (Cheval Blanc produces wines that are an exception to this, blending with rich Merlot grown on unique land and given rigorous small-oak-cask treatment.)

find something less recherché. Yapp Bros of Mere can supply good examples, and Peter Dominic list a red Saumur, though it's a less pure specimen.

If you see the word Cabernet on an Italian wine label, then it is almost certainly predominantly Cabernet Franc, planted much more widely there than Cabernet Sauvignon. Friuli and Trentino-Alto Adige, up to the far north-east, turn out very good-value wines of this type.

Northern Italian Cabernets are becoming increasingly easy to find on British shelves, and they're very good value too. Note that they seem rather sweeter than Loire Cabernets, because they're ripened by a bit more sun. These are red wines that can be drunk with great relish in their youth.

There are many similarities between them, but you should be able to recognize a Cabernet Franc from a Cabernet Sauvignon by its lower tannin, colour and body. When Cabernet Sauvignon is cultivated in a very cool climate, however, it starts to taste remarkably like Cabernet Franc (see New Zealand). Miguel Torres stoutly maintains that much of the 'Cabernet Sauvignon' planted in Chile is in fact Cabernet Franc.

Try to taste one of the Loire or Italian Cabernets alongside a Cabernet Sauvignon of the same age, a young Médoc or Graves perhaps. Taste the Claret second because its much higher tannin content will pucker up your mouth, leaving a coating of astringency all over it. Notice how much more body and colour the Claret has too – and surely it seems drier?

The Torres red Santa Digna from Chile is an interesting example of a South American Cabernet Franc, available from La Vigneronne of London SW7. Compare it with a Conchay Toro Cabernet, also from Chile, and see if you can discern the different characteristics of a Cabernet Sauvignon in the second wine. Also look at a wine labelled Cabernet Sauvignon from NZ if you can find one (try Averys of Bristol). See how Cabernet Franc-like the distance from the Equator makes it.

Merlot the fruitcake varietal, and yields

Merlot is to St Emilion and Pomerol what Cabernet Sauvignon is to Médoc and Graves. The varietal that predominates on this 'right bank' is a wonderfully attractive supple sort of grape which, when properly vinified, turns out rich, spicy wines with all the plummy sort of appeal of a rich fruitcake. So appealing can it be, in fact, that Pomerol's Château Pétrus, made almost entirely of Merlot, qualifies for the dubious distinction of being the world's most expensive wine. The very joy of wine.

It shouldn't be too difficult to find a good, toothsome example of a Merlot-based Claret. Any St Emilion would do, as indeed would any wine that has St Emilion on the label in any form (there are all sorts of complicated and tiny 'appellations' such as Montagne-St Emilion, St Georges-St Emilion, and various other hyphenated communes). A Pomerol would be even better, being likely to contain a higher proportion of Merlot, as explained below. Most off-licences should be able to offer a 'petit château' (i.e. not reckoned officially 'grand' in terms of quality, but perfectly sound). Corney & Barrow of London EC1 specialize in top quality properties from St Emilion and Pomerol; you could even buy yourself a Château Petrus from them.

It ripens easily and produces wines that taste quite sweet. This counterbalances what tannin there may be to make them seem much softer than would an equivalent Cabernet Sauvignon. A good Merlot-based wine often has a sort of rich velvety texture with a heady, complex aroma that some have variously described as gunshot, pheasant and gamey. I'm spirited more to the spice shelf than the game parlour myself.

Notice the greater viscosity and slightly higher alcohol content in a Merlot than in a Cabernet Sauvignon. There's a warm, sunbaked sort of flavour that is reminiscent of very ripe fruit, almost a plummy fruitcake. The tannin seems less marked than in Cabernet Sauvignon, and there's much more richness than in Cabernet Franc.

Merlot reaches its apogee in St Emilion and Pomerol. However, plantings are increasing dramatically on the US west coast as Californian winemakers are realizing what the potential is for a rich alternative to their darling Cabernet Sauvignon. Further north and east in Washington is one of the very few wine regions that have taken to Merlot in a serious way and the state is turning out very attractive supple

Look out for Merlots from Stag's Leap, Newton and Duckhorn in California, Château Ste Michelle in Washington and Sokol Blosser in Oregon. La Vigneronne, the Wine Studio and Lay & Wheeler of Colchester may be able to help. The California vintages I have tasted – all fairly early in the west-coast career of the Merlot grape – are very high in tannin, but this may well be reduced by winemakers during the examples, some of them vinified in Oregon.

1980s. Washington and Oregon Merlots are softer, gentler and designed for much earlier consumption. Notice the same sweet fruity nose, however.

Merlot, like Cabernet Franc, has long been planted in the north of Italy, with very variable results. It is almost inconceivable that Château Pétrus should emanate from the same varietal as some of Italy's cheaper 'two-litre' Merlots. Comparison of St Emilion/Pomerol with such a wine illustrates well the result of asking too much of a vine in terms of grape production. There are stringent controls on most French *appellations* as to exactly how much wine each acre of vines may produce. A good property may well do an additional summer prune to further restrict yield (*rendement*) to make only, say, 30 hectolitres of wine per hectare (about 2½ acres). An Italian Merlot designated *vino da tavola* may have been made to about three or four times this yield, and the taste is obviously 'stretched' accordingly. The result is a much thinner, less exciting wine, although there are also likely to be variables other than yield of course – climate and clone being the two obvious ones. There are good Italian Merlots; look for the DOC ones of the north.

Compare your St Emilion or Pomerol standard Merlot example with an inexpensive Italian specimen. Many licensed supermarkets and unexciting off-licences stock one, often in a big screwtop bottle. You can tell just from the colour that the Italian specimen is much thinner and paler. It will taste that way too with pronounced acidity spun out over a rather watery taste. A pale (red) colour, often rather dull, is an indication that the vine yield was too high for quality.

Good, exciting Italian Merlots can be found with 'DOC' on the label (the Italian equivalent of 'appellation contrôlée') from all over northern Italy. Victoria Wine may have one from Villa Ronche in Friuli.

Claret – a geography lesson

Bordeaux is a very obligingly well-ordered wine region, which is why it is such a favourite with those who enjoy blind tasting. It's divided into separate estates or châteaux which don't change (much) from year to year. Each region – Médoc, Graves, St Emilion, Pomerol and the lesser ones – is divided into neat communes, each of which should have their own characteristics just as each vintage puts its own stamp on to the wines it produces. This is particularly true in the biggest top-quality Claret region, the Médoc.

When tasting a Claret blind, the taster would first of all decide whether he was faced with primarily Merlot (St Emilion/Pomerol) or Cabernet (Médoc/Graves). If he smelt the rich plumminess of Merlot, he would look for great intense spiciness that suggested *lots* of it – with a deep colour – and that would lead him to Pomerol. If the Merlot seemed to have been mixed with a noticeable proportion of Cabernet Franc (alias Bouchet) producing a lightish-hued, slightly farmyard-smelling wine, then this would suggest St Emilion.

In a wine that seemed predominantly Cabernet Sauvignon he would look for the distinctive 'texture', a sort of dry, sandy, almost earthy taste that is characteristic of Graves. If he didn't find it, he should in theory start trying to work out which of the Médoc communes or parishes the wine could come from. (In practice, most blind tasters are casting about wildly by this stage. Could be Italy? California perhaps? Oh for a logical brain and cool soul in these circumstances!) Neatly, the most northerly commune, St Estèphe, produces the wines highest in acidity. (The Napa Valley plays a nasty trick on wine tasters, with its coolest vineyards and most acid wines in the south nearest the Equator, but also nearer the cooling influence of San Francisco Bay than the warmer vineyards to the north.)

Wines from St Estèphe can be hard and very tannic when young. Pauillac is the most famous commune, with three of the four Médoc 'first growths' classified in 1855. Its wines tend to be very concentrated and blackcurranty with lots of tannin. Margaux is quite a way to the south and wines made there tend to be softer and slightly more Merloty. St Julien contains lots of second-growth châteaux and, typically, makes wines that come somewhere between Pauillac and Margaux – 'just enough of everything' is the convenient description, though a certain cedarwood flavour is associated with the commune.

This amount of detail is given here because Claret guessing games are the most common and can, believe it or not, be great fun. I suspect that those who indulge in them have more faith than I in just how likely they are to be right. I've seen it rarely, but it's the getting there that's fun.

see diagram overleaf

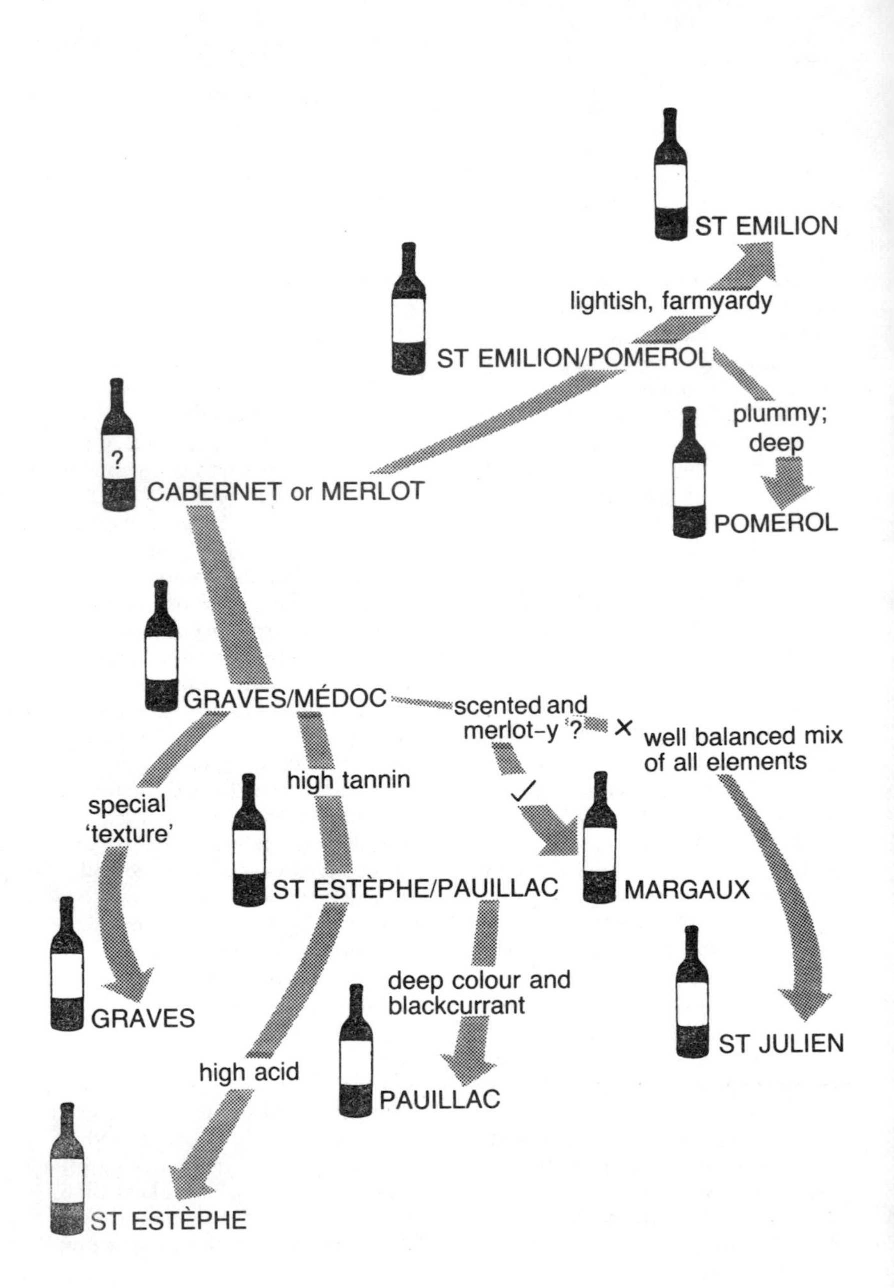
ST EMILION
lightish, farmyardy
ST EMILION/POMEROL
plummy; deep
POMEROL
?
CABERNET or MERLOT
GRAVES/MÉDOC
scented and merlot-y ?
✓
×
well balanced mix of all elements
special 'texture'
high tannin
ST ESTÈPHE/PAUILLAC
MARGAUX
GRAVES
deep colour and blackcurrant
ST JULIEN
high acid
PAUILLAC
ST ESTÈPHE

Vintage and age

If guessing-the-commune seems a dazzlingly skilful dinner-party trick, guessing-the-vintage assumes almost mystical status. Contrary to popular belief, there are relatively few sorts of wine in which such a feat makes sense. All the dry, crisp whites we drink with relish when they're young tend to follow the same path towards a stale unexciting state with years, so that guessing the vintage for most whites equates with guessing the age. The same is true of many of the less exciting reds that are sold in huge volumes to be drunk as young as possible.

Guessing the vintage is significant only for wines that develop interesting characteristics with age, i.e. those that mature rather than simply age, and are made in regions where the weather varies sufficiently from year to year to give each vintage its own character. This means that vintage-guessing is a widespread exercise only for white wines based on Chardonnay, Riesling and Sémillon and reds from Cabernet Sauvignon, Merlot and most of the other varietals discussed below. We touched on the great years for the three white varieties with ageing potential, but it is with Claret, again, that most fun can be had with vintage guessing. California Cabernets do vary from vintage to vintage (the question being whether they were made in a drought year or a year immediately post-drought, rather than in a wash-out), but the much more temperate climate of Bordeaux fashions the most dramatic vintage variations.

Chardonnay – White Burgundy

1982 Goodish quality, still very acid.
1981 Good, but not destined for greater things.
1980 High in acidity and often low in fruit.
1979 Very fine, starting to develop.
1978 Excellent, with lots of body.
1977 Pretty mean, with very marked acidity.
1976 Very strange; too ripe, if anything, and already golden.

Chardonnay – California

1982 Higher acids and lower alcohol than average; almost European.
1981 Fast maturing and rich.
1980 Rich, concentrated and (some) very beefy indeed.
1979 Very ripe but with balancing acidity.
1978 Lots of alcohol and already golden; some with great potential.
1977 Concentrated flavours still developing.
1976 Drought kept alcohol up and acid down.

Riesling – Germany

Vintages with Riesling are really interesting only if wines of Spätlese quality and above are produced in any quantity. At the time of writing (1983) the last such vintages were 1976 and 1975, though 1979 produced some attractive Mosel Auslesen and a few fine bottles from Rheinpfalz and Nahe.

1976 Very sweet and heavy rich wines, already turning golden.
1975 Less unctuous than 1976 and possibly better balanced for long life.

Opposite are brief vintage notes for the various wines mentioned so far. They should be useful for some time, but are only outlines and won't last for ever. There is no shortage of literature on this subject, and the monthly magazine *Decanter* (St John's Chambers, 2–10 St John's Road, London SW11) regularly prints up-to-date assessments of characteristics of wines as they develop. It is important to realize, by the way, that vintages evolve. A vintage such as 1975 was hailed as 'vintage of the century' as it was being picked. Before it was ten years old, doubts were being expressed about it being just too tannic for its own good. Doubtless there will be a change of accepted opinion, for better or worse, by the end of this century.

However, it is worth studying a specific example of just how different two consecutive vintages can be. We have seen that red wines lose colour and start to go browner with age, but there is much more to identifying Claret vintages than guessing age. The 1980 vintage, for instance, was a poor thin thing set between two very useful, fruity, well-coloured ones. Looking at a 1980 compared with a 1979 you might be tempted to think it was older, so pale will it be in comparison. Look at the actual hue. The 1980 is still fairly purplish and therefore can't be all that old. When you taste it, however, you see that it is very light in body and high in youthful acidity. The 1979 wine is much more concentrated in both colour and flavour, still with noticeable tannin. Even though it is a relatively 'forward' vintage, the

Riesling – California

Wine styles with this grape have been evolving so fast here that, in the history of west-coast Johannisberg Riesling, vintage characteristics are less important than winery and date.

Riesling – Australia

Even though so far away, 1976 was the 'annus mirabilis' for Riesling in South Australia as well as in Germany, though 1977 was very successful in Clare-Watervale.

Sémillon – Bordeaux

1982 Both dry and sweet wines are attractive, but too low in acid to keep.
1980 Lots of fruit and acidity, with botrytis on the sweet wines.
1979 Fine, lightish and a bit of botrytis on the sweet ones.
1978 Full bodied and rich, even the dry ones.
1977 Hardly any Sauternes and very tart dry white Bordeaux.
1976 Lots of sunshine, ripeness and body in dry and sweet; golden.
1975 More acidity and, as in Germany, possibly better keepers than 1976.

Semillon – Australia

1981 would be a good year to taste for youthful greatness, and then to keep.

Cabernet Sauvignon – California

1982 Youthful and with marked acidity for this combination of grape and climate.
1981 Lightish and early maturing, with lower tannin than average.
1980 Very big, with lots of fruit and tannin.

1979 still has a few years to go before it softens.

Still talking Claret, if you find a wine with very deep colour indeed it is likely to be one of the following: 1982, 1978, 1975 or 1970. If the wine is very pale, it is either very old (if it's browny or tawny) or (if it's still definitely red) it will probably be from the 1980, 1977 or 1973 vintages.

Remember that, with red wines, tannin and depth of colour are an indication of youth, while complexity of flavour and fading of hue suggest maturity. If you have bought a quantity of the same wine, a case of a dozen bottles for instance, you will want to monitor its progress so that you don't drink it too soon. With a moderate quality Claret, the wine might be ready to drink within three to five years of the vintage, while the most revered names can take three decades to mature. Generally speaking, the better the wine, the longer you will have to wait before it can prove it. The sadness is, of course, that you can never know when a wine has reached its peak of quality until it has passed it. Again in general terms, Cabernet Sauvignon wines take longer to mature than those based on Merlot and/or Cabernet Franc.

Also bear in mind that young Claret sometimes goes through a stage they call 'dumb', meaning that it doesn't say anything much to your senses, particularly your nose. Especially when recently bottled, about two years after the vintage, good quality Claret can seem very closed up, as though it's turning in on itself to

1979 Patchy; some very thin (for California) wines.
1978 Very, very rich; sometimes too much alcohol and body.
1977 Some very good and not too heavy.
1976 Very strange – even more tannin than usual.
1975 Lighter than average, but some very good.
1974 Massive; impressive for quantity, if not quality, of sensations.

Anything earlier you are unlikely to find, either here or in the USA.

Claret – Bordeaux (Cabernet Sauvignon, Cabernet Franc and Merlot)

1982 So far, looks wonderful. Everything there in concentration.
1981 Good colour and fruit; lowish on tannin and acidity; attractive already.
1980 Light in colour and body, with a bit too much acidity.
1979 Very supple and easy with lots of fruit; St Emilion/Pomerol very good.
1978 A 'classic' vintage with lots of everything, including tannin; still closed, but should develop very well.
1977 A little hard and always light, with marked acidity; fruitier than many 1980s.
1976 Seen as too blowsy to be great; lots of fruit and a certain sweet ripeness, but a little bit hollow and not much tannin; good Merlot.
1975 Another classic; very concentrated and with marked tannin; many wines are so hard, even after eight years, that fears have been voiced for their future.
1974 Still too little fruit for the tannin in many instances.

concentrate on knitting together all the various elements inside the bottle. Don't write off a Claret that is very deep coloured and tannic but without much bouquet. It's probably merely youthful and getting ready to reveal its charms.

1973 Soft, fruity, light and without tannin and acid to preserve them; useful as a vintage to drink young (like 1976); now fading.

1972 Too much acid and tannin and too little fruit in most cases; hard and tart now.

1971 Easy and quite soft; some very good St Emilion/Pomerols.

1970 A proven classic; lots of everything; very deep colour, lots of body and fruit, plus the tannin to keep the wines into the next century.

Other great or very good vintages were 1966, 1962, 1961 and 1955.

Red wine + oak = Rioja

Oak maturation is much more important for red wines than for whites. Many producers of red wines would like to have rows of neat new small oak casks in their cellars for the extra dimensions of flavour they could add to their wines. What prevents them is the cost of the casks themselves, and the work involved in keeping them in good shape. Wine evaporates fast when it's kept in a porous wooden container, and cellarmen have to work constantly keeping each cask topped up so that air won't get to work on the wine and spoil it to the point of oxidation. Wood also encourages the natural precipitation of the bits of solid matter left in suspension in the wine after fermentation. A good thing – except that the wine has to be regularly pumped, or 'racked', off this deposit to stop it taking on a stale taste. This means that wine in a well-kept cellar is always being moved from one cask to another,

Wine from the wood definitely tastes different

leaving behind casks that need careful cleaning and reconditioning. No wonder the coopers of France are turning to California as the most obvious place to find winemakers spurred on by fanaticism to such hard work.

In a well kept cellar wine is always kept moving from one cask to another

The alternatives to wooden casks are large vats made of stainless steel and other inert substances, which are free from the dangers of evaporation and much easier to clean. Wines kept in such vats for the period of settling and 'marrying' after fermentation taste simpler and much more obviously fruity than those which take on the layer of oak flavouring offered by wood storage. There are some wines that are much better suited to this sort of treatment though, and they would be rather overpowered by oak. Beaujolais and other light fruity wines, such as Valpolicella, are obvious examples.

Claret, as usual, provides an excellent illustration of the effect of oak ageing. All classed growth properties will put their wines into small oak casks, the traditional Bordeaux 225-litre *barrique*, as will many châteaux which although not *classés* are making serious wine for a medium to long life. The better regarded the property, the newer the casks they can afford, the more intense oak flavour will be picked up, and the longer we have to wait until the wine is drinkably mature. There are some Clarets that are specifically designed for a vivacious youth rather than an august old age. They and wood are kept firmly apart so that the fresh fruit quality of the wine is emphasized and the liquid is ready to drink only a year or so after

You can use your 'standard Cabernet Sauvignon' example to illustrate the combination of oak and red Bordeaux. Choose any wine from the Médoc or Graves, preferably one that is from a specific château. To contrast with this, try to track down either Belair Claret from Sichel or one of Pierre Coste's youthful Graves, sold by Adnams of Southwold. Notice that the second wine, which has been kept in an inert material, is very fruity and the tannin is hardly noticeable. The first wine, unless so old it will have cost you well over £15, is much more tannic, and probably also has a much more complicated flavour. Underneath the cedary oakiness of the first wine is the straightforward fruitiness of the second, but the two wines are as the vintage. Compare one of each type to study the effect of Bordeaux's eighteen months or so in small oak casks.

dissimilar as Barolo and Beaujolais.

Perhaps a cheaper way of 'tasting oak' on red wines is via a bottle from Greece. A high proportion of the red wines exported from there have a distinctive oaky flavour as a result of their treatment.

The number of times an oak cask has been used before affects the final taste of the wine, as outlined already in Chapter 1. The newer a cask, the more flavour and tannin it has to give to the wine. The lesser properties of Bordeaux put their wines into casks that have perhaps already been used by several smarter châteaux, and the effects of keeping wines in wood like this are therefore much less obvious.

Try to compare a 'petit château' Claret (perhaps one carrying either the 'appellation' Bordeaux or one of the outlying regions such as Bourg, Blaye or Premières Côtes de Bordeaux) with a better quality château, either one that is 'classé' or one described as 'bourgeois' on the label – i.e. one rung down from the 1855 classes. You will note much more flavour on the superior wine, with an intense tannic flavour brought about by its newer and more vigorous oak lodgings during infancy.

The exact provenance of the oak also has a great bearing on the flavour of any wine kept in cask. Limousin and Nevers are the standard sorts of oak used in Bordeaux. You can taste their rather taut, dry, rigorous flavour in your standard Cabernet Sauvignon example. Californians have exhibited awesome enthusiasm in experimenting with different sorts of oak (and different depths of char, *and* different sorts of stave). They have found that there is a great difference in flavour between the native American oak and various imported French varieties. Most top wineries try to use small oak casks for their top Cabernets, though the much cheaper American oak gives an easy, sweet vanilla flavour to lesser wines.

Examine a red Rioja. An example shouldn't be difficult to find. (Only beware of the very young Riojas that have been shipped to this country in recent years.) Make sure it has a vintage date of more than three years before, and have a look at the seal on the back of the bottle. They seem always to be changing the regulations, but at the last count 'vino de crianza' wines must have at least one year in wood, 'reservas' at least two and 'gran reservas' between two and five years. In practice, CUNE and La Rioja Alta produce very good Riojas, though almost any supermarket Rioja will do to illustrate the point. Notice the pale red colour with a slight tawny tinge. There should never be any sediment in a Rioja, so often has it been racked off its lees. Now take a sniff. There's warmth, sweetness and vanilla there (and sometimes even a slight suggestion of vomit, I'm afraid, though not on the better examples). Take note of how different this opulent vanilla American-oak smell is from the taut cedar French-oak flavour on a fine young Claret.

We in Britain are obviously rather keen on American oak. Rioja, the warm red wine from northern Spain, has been a great success here and its chief flavour component is American oak. All red Rioja with the *crianza* seal on the back has spent some time in small American oak casks – usually two years or more, and certainly usually long enough to give the wine the very distinctive sweet vanilla smell. Red Rioja must be one of the easiest wines to recognize – not because of the grape, for most Riojas are made of a blend of several local grape varieties, but by the American oak flavour that is its keynote. Another good clue to a Rioja's identity is its relatively light colour, made paler by the Riojan practice of moving wine from cask to cask, or 'racking', even more often than in most wine regions.

Some white Rioja is given a similar American oak treatment, though an increasing proportion is now made without any wood so that it tastes like a cross between a Muscadet and a Mâcon Blanc. The 'traditional' white Riojas demonstrate well how white wines gain rather than lose colour with oak ageing, and can have an interesting mixture of the vanilla bouquet and fairly high acidity. Again, they are made of a mixture of local Spanish grapes.

Marques de Murrieta and white Tondonia Lopez de Heredia are good examples of the traditional white Rioja style, while Marques de Caceres exemplifies the new crisp one. Spanish specialists include Laymont & Shaw of Truro and the Sherston Wine Company. Being both dry and rich, these wines resemble some mature dry white Graves.

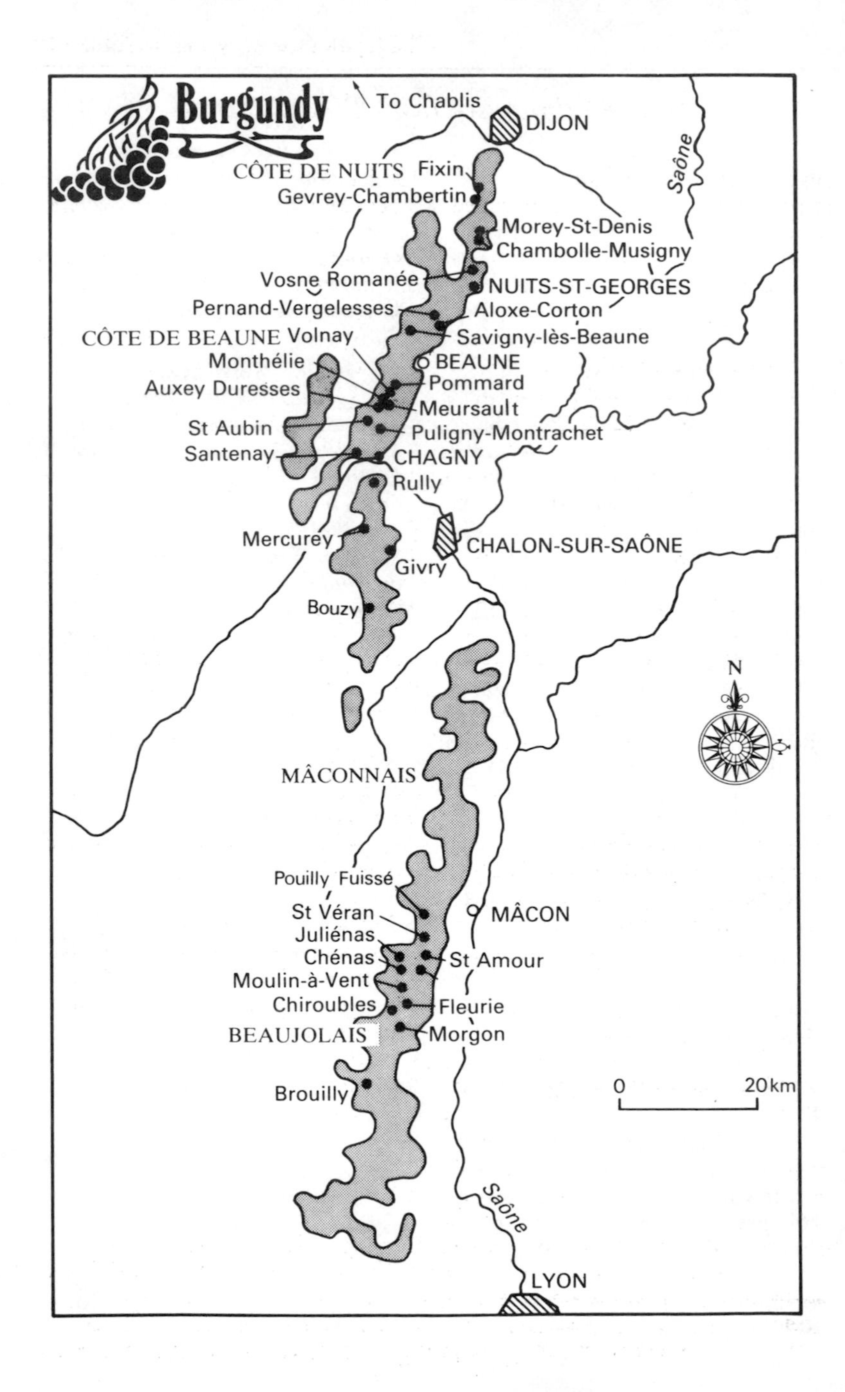
Burgundy
To Chablis
DIJON
Saône
CÔTE DE NUITS
Fixin
Gevrey-Chambertin
Morey-St-Denis
Chambolle-Musigny
Vosne Romanée
NUITS-ST-GEORGES
Pernand-Vergelesses
Aloxe-Corton
CÔTE DE BEAUNE
Volnay
Savigny-lès-Beaune
Monthélie
BEAUNE
Pommard
Auxey Duresses
Meursault
St Aubin
Puligny-Montrachet
Santenay
CHAGNY
Rully
Mercurey
CHALON-SUR-SAÔNE
Givry
Bouzy
N
MÂCONNAIS
Pouilly Fuissé
St Véran
MÂCON
Juliénas
Chénas
St Amour
Moulin-à-Vent
Chiroubles
Fleurie
BEAUJOLAIS
Morgon
Brouilly
0
20km
Saône
LYON

The fabulously fussy Pinot Noir

Just as Cabernet Sauvignon is responsible for most of the great red wines of Bordeaux, Pinot Noir is solely responsible for all the great red Burgundies. No red grape other than Pinot is allowed into such *appellations* as Gevrey-Chambertin, Chambolle-Musigny, Clos de Vougeot, Romanée-Conti, Nuits-St-Georges, Aloxe-Corton, Beaune, Pommard and Volnay. When grown in the finest vineyards of the famous Côte d'Or, the 'golden slope' of Burgundy, in a good year and vinified by a careful winemaker, it can produce fabulous wine. 'Ethereal', 'soft and velvety', 'iron hand in a velvet glove', 'rich and scented' are all descriptions of great red Burgundy. 'Overpriced', 'thin and mean', 'ludicrously light' are all descriptions of bottles of red Burgundy that have disappointed.

It is a sad fact that red Burgundy offers more disappointments more expensively than any other wine type. This is partly because too many wines have been made by men who are good at growing vines but not necessarily at making wine; partly because some very poor clones of Pinot have been planted; partly because the region produces much less than world demand, so can get away with offering poor value; and partly because the Pinot Noir is such a finicky grape. The Cabernet Sauvignon has travelled happily all over the world, with some stupendous results. But winemakers and vine growers from Napa to New Zealand try each year to make a presentable Pinot – and usually fail

For the taste of true Pinot fruit you would be well advised to go for one of the lesser 'appellations' of Burgundy. Not only do they cost a fraction of the big names, they are also usually more reliable (at their quality level). These aren't wines for great development, but the well-made ones offer good simple Pinot flavour. Plain old 'appellation' Bourgogne (French for Burgundy) is a good one to head for. Louis Jadot's Réserve Couvent des Jacobins is reasonably priced for the quality, and available from Victoria Wine. Aubert de Villaine's La Digoine is a very pure Bourgogne Rouge and available from Adnams of Southwold and the Bow Wine Vaults of London EC4. Notice that the wines are fairly light and have a very fruity nose – it reminds me of raspberries, other people of violets. There's something soft and sweet about the wine, and little tannin (though there may be quite a lot of acidity in a not-so-good vintage, because the region is so far north).

Probably the cheapest way of tasting Pinot Noir is via a bottle of a sweet red Bulgarian wine sold by Victoria Wine called Balkan Prince. The flavour won't be the purest, but it's a start.

dismally. Good Pinot can be so exasperatingly great that attempts will continue to be made (and with any luck quality in Burgundy will rise) so it is worth getting your palate trained to recognize the grape.

Take time to 'monitor' just how you feel after swallowing wine

Good Pinot is slightly sweet and definitely more gently perfumed than the rather uncompromising Cabernet. Tannin is much less marked, for Pinot skins are in general much thinner. This also accounts for the Pinot's relatively light colour (though very serious places, such as the ultra-pricey Domaine de la Romanée Conti, ferment the wine on the skins for so long that they manage to extract quite a good depth of colour). Most Pinots have less body than the average Cabernet and their appeal is perhaps more subtle. It is easy to see why Claret was always described as masculine and Burgundy as feminine, however much one resists such facile descriptions. Some tasters describe the scent of Pinot as boiled beetroot, others as dead game. In young Pinot there's the very definite smell of raspberries, while in middle age it takes on definite vegetal overtones. I sometimes smell meat and two veg!

The Côte d'Or is made up of the northern part, the Côte de Nuits centred on Nuits-St-Georges, and the southern Côte de Beaune dominated by the town of Beaune. Traditionally, the wines of the Côte de Nuits are visualized as firmer and longer lasting than the softer, lighter style of the Côte de Beaune. In practice, the name of the producer is a much better guide to likely style and quality than even the name of the *appellation*. All of these wines are

Only a handful of wine merchants in Britain treat Burgundy seriously, and it can be very difficult indeed to find genuine examples of Côte d'Or reds. The following should be able to help you spend your money wisely: Adnams of Southwold, Averys of Bristol, Corney & Barrow of London EC1, Gerard Harris of Aston Clinton, Laytons of London NW1, Lay & Wheeler of Colchester, O. W. Loeb of London SW1 and Henry Townsend of Amersham.

expensive, but if you have lots of money and patience you can build up your own impressions of the different producers. The briefest of brief outlines of mine are shown opposite.

The most exciting provenance of Côte d'Or Burgundy is the individual 'domaine', provided it is one that is quality conscious. The route to them is through one of the British wine merchants listed above. Most of Burgundy's output is, however, bottled by the shippers or 'négociants' and they have very varying reputations. Here are some of my favourites for red wine:

Bouchard Père et Fils – good vineyards around Beaune.
Chanson – very light but elegant wines.
Joseph Drouhin – extremely rigorous, the best of the new methods grafted on to traditional techniques.
Louis Jadot – rich and firm.
Louis Latour – solid, even better for whites.

Much cheaper than those from the Côte d'Or, and usually rather light and tart, are the wines from its upper hinterland, Hautes Côtes de Nuits and Beaune. Rather better examples of affordable red Burgundy made from the Pinot grape come from the Côte Chalonnaise to the south. Rully, Givry and Mercurey are the names to look for here. Any further south and you are into Gamay country. The grape that makes such luscious wines in the Beaujolais region turns out some very ordinary stuff under the name of Mâcon Rouge, geographically between the Côte Chalonnaise and Beaujolais. The explanation may be partly clonal.

Peter Dominic and Justerini & Brooks have made a speciality of the Chalonnaise wines, especially the ones of the excellent producer Delorme. Notice that they are definitely lighter and leaner than fine Côte d'Or wines, in terms of style and quality a halfway house between the Côte d'Or and the Hautes Côtes.

Vintages for red Burgundy are even more variable than for red Bordeaux, and indeed considerably more

Recent vintages for red Burgundy

1982 Difficult.
1981 Light and lacking fruit.

variable than for white Burgundy. Chardonnay is a much less fussy vine than the delicate Pinot Noir. So far north is Burgundy that the Pinot ripens there satisfactorily only about one vintage in three, and until recently rot has been a severe problem. The 1975 vintage, for instance, was a memorial to the poor colour and stale flavour that can affect the resultant wine after rot has struck grapes in the vineyard. However, in a fine vintage, such as 1978, the grapes ripen fully to produce lots of sugar (and therefore alcohol and body), colour and flavour. Pinots in general are ready to drink long before Cabernets, owing to their lower tannin content and lighter weight.

1980 Some finely balanced wines.
1979 Lots of attractive fruit, for early drinking.
1978 Very lively with lots of body and fruit; less tannic than 1976.
1977 Good colour but too much acidity.
1976 Enormous, with lots of tannin too. When will they soften?
1975 Thin, rotten and not properly ripe.
1974 Good colour but dull.
1973 Easy fruity current drinking.
1972 Marked acidity but lots of ripe fruit too; good structure.
1971 Superlative; all elements are there.

True Pinot is a fairly light wine, but many readers may be surprised by this description. For years Britons have been accustomed to Burgundies that are heavy and soupy, with a dark ruby colour and so much weight they could be described as positively gutsy. This is because it was not until 1973 that the laws prohibiting the addition of fuller wines from the south had to be obeyed in this country. Long after the French had accustomed themselves to true Burgundy without the prop of Algerian and, later, Rhône and Italian blending wines, we were being sold these *mélanges* as 'Burgundy'. When controls got more stringent prices rocketed, and it seems an age since I've seen names like Volnay and Pommard on wine lists in this country. Some merchants specialize in 'old style' Burgundy. Exactly how, I know not.

Berry Bros & Rudd of St James's, London SW1, still list some full-bodied, almost jammy Burgundies of yesteryear. Look especially for the pre-1973 ones that won't have the magic words 'appellation contrôlée' on the label, if you hanker after Burgundies past.

For years Britons have been accustomed to Burgundys that are heavy & syrupy

Some Pinot Noir is grown in other parts of north-eastern France: in Alsace (where it produces a dark rosé, illustrating well how difficult it is to get a deep-coloured Pinot even in a region whose white wines regularly notch up 13° alcohol); in Sancerre, where it is responsible for all those Sancerre rouges and rosés; and in Champagne, where it constitutes about one third of the blend that goes into the sparkling wine. Pure Pinot is available as a still wine of Champagne sold as Coteaux Champenois rouge, and the villages of Bouzy and Cumières are famous for it. The Pinot Noir grown there is supplemented by the rather fruitier but less distinguished Pinot Meunier, rarely encountered elsewhere – though I have tasted as a 100 per cent varietal Pinot Meunier made by Great Western in Australia.

Very little Alsace Pinot is imported into Britain, so keen are the German tourists who flood the region to take home a bottle of red wine. However, Sancerre Rouge is stocked by upmarket shops like Harrods and Fields of London SW3. Most examples demonstrate a bit of Pinot scent, and a very light colour. They are usually chaptalized fairly heavily to bring them up to a toothsome alcoholic strength. If you ever find a Champagne that is described as a Blanc de Noirs (Bollinger occasionally make one from their intense and ancient Vieilles Vignes of Pinot) it will be pure Pinot, as is the irresistibly named Bouzy Rouge.

The most successful Pinots produced outside Burgundy have been grown in very cool micro-climates within much warmer regions. The Chalone winery, 2,000 feet up in the Santa Lucia mountains of California, has produced that state's best examples to date, and there is no shortage of seekers after the sublime Pinot there. The cooler climes of Oregon to the north have been tipped to rival Burgundy eventually, and the Eyrie Vineyard has made great progress towards that goal. Less successful American examples are too obviously 'hot climate' and are too plummy and full-blown to benefit from the delicacy that Pinot can give. The same criticism can be levelled at most attempts in Australia, though Tyrrell's (much to their surprise) won acclaim at the Paris 'Wine Olympics' of 1979.

La Vigneronne of London SW7, The Wine Studio of London SW1 and Les Amis du Vin of London W1 carry a wide range of California wines. Notice how rich and plummy most of these Pinots are, reared in California sunshine; in some cases the vegetable flavour almost is so ripe it's almost rotten but there's no shortage of sugar and (rather brownish) colour. Chalone and Trefethen have thrilled me the most so far. Averys occasionally have stocks of Tyrrell Pinot, which to me has that volcanic twang of Australia's Hunter Valley. They also have Nobilo's New Zealand Pinot Noir, which has much of the true Pinot scent to it, with the firmness that nearly two years in small Limousin casks can give the grape. In the Torres wine, on the other hand, notice how the oak treatment has rather overwhelmed

Nobilo make a very attractive Pinot in New Zealand, where the climate perhaps most nearly duplicates that of Burgundy. Other Pinots which can give a great deal of pleasure and help to imprint the flavour of the grape at not too great a price come from Italy and Spain. Torres make Pinot Noir the dominant character of their rather hefty, oaky Santa Magdala, and certainly there's a good Pinot scent, even though the wine could hardly be described as delicate. The Pinot Nero of northern Italy is also based on Pinot Noir, called Blauburgunder in the Tyrolean part of the country where it is most successful – just as it is in both Austria and Germany, where it turns out very thin stuff indeed. It is also grown in Hungary, where it's best as 'Villanyi Burgundi'.

the fruit, and that the smell of Pinot is followed by something just a bit too much like matchsticks and not much like raspberries.

Note, in all these examples, the effect of climate on the highly susceptible Pinot Noir grape. In the cool north of Europe it seems so much lighter and more acid than when reared in the sunshine of California and Australia.

Common in South Africa is a beefy red grape called Pinotage which is a cross between Pinot Noir and Cinsaut, the rough and vigorous southern Rhône grape. In my view, the Cinsaut is now by far the dominant strain, and the Pinot leaves only a certain residual sweetness to remember it by. The wines are good value, though, for those who want a hearty alternative to Châteauneuf (*not* to Chambertin).

Collison's of SW1 and the Cape Wine Centres of London and Edinburgh will have a few examples of Pinotage. They have the same sweetness as Pinot Noir, plus something that's almost inky. But these are rugby players – true Pinot can play nothing tougher than the violin.

A milestone tasting exercise

Here follows an exercise so important it deserves a section all to itself. Outsiders might think that telling Claret from red Burgundy is absurdly simple – until you've blindfolded them and proved they can't even tell red from white.

You can do this exercise with any Claret and any red Burgundy, though it makes sense to choose a pair of roughly the same age and quality. If you know you're faced with a Château Mouton-Rothschild 1961 and a supermarket's non-vintage

One friend of mine marked her newly won status as Master of Wine by identifying a Burgundy as a Claret at the celebratory dinner. Famous gastronome André Simon offered comfort to us all with his reply when asked when he'd last mistaken Claret for Burgundy. 'Oh, not since lunch,' he smiled.

If you can master this classic test of wine expertise you should be justly proud of yourself.

(NV) Burgundy, you really are making life a bit easy for yourself. Any of the wines suggested so far would do; your example of Pinot and Cabernet would make a particularly good pair. (You might find Merlot-based Clarets more difficult to distinguish from Pinot because both grapes are quite sweet.)

Here is a crude outline of your deductions in the order you're likely to make them:

COLOUR	*pale* *Pinot, or Cab in poor year*	*deep* *Cab, or Pinot in very good year*
VISCOSITY	*low* *Pinot*	*high* *Cab or heavily chaptalized Pinot*
FLAVOUR	*raspberries / vegetables* *Pinot*	*blackcurrants / cedar / herbaceous* *Cabernet*
SWEETNESS	*sweet* *Pinot, or Cab in opulent year*	*dry* *Cabernet*
ACIDITY	*marked* *Pinot, or very young (or ancient) Cab*	*swamped by fruit* *Cabernet*
TANNIN	*low* *Pinot, or very mature Cabernet*	*high* *youthful Cabernet*
BODY	*light* *Pinot, or very poor Cab*	*full* *Cabernet, or Pinot from exceptional vintage*

Now you could try to distinguish between a St Emilion or Pomerol and a red Burgundy. The Merlot-based wine will also have sweetness, but it's a plummy sort of richness in a full-bodied tannic wine with lots of colour, whereas red Burgundies are more likely to offer a raspberry sort of fruitiness in a wine that is

Note that it helps here, as so often, to have an accomplice to feed you an unidentified glass of each. It is wise to keep the glasses in the same relation to each other, so that your accomplice knows that the glass on the left, say, is always the Claret. Or they can mark the glasses with a felt-tip pen. If you have (or prefer) to lighter in both colour and body.

perform this feat solo, you can do it by switching the glasses round and round so that eventually you forget which is which. The trouble is that you can't top up in the middle of the exercise, and you need to have learnt enough to be able to match each glass to the contents of the bottles when the work is over.

Syrah, black as night

In Europe the Syrah grape is largely confined to two small strips of steep vineyard on the banks of the northern Rhône just south of Lyons, where it produces wines called Hermitage, Crozes Hermitage, Côte Rôtie, St Joseph and Cornas. It's reassuringly easy to recognize by its very dark, almost black colour and its high level of tannin. The wines are concentrated and chewy and have a distinctive 'essence-of-something' flavour that I now associate with burnt rubber, though some people think of tar or ink. (It is a measure of how difficult it is to match words with flavours that so many of the expressions we use to describe wines we like seem uncomplimentary.)

A first-class and not too expensive way to acquaint yourself with well-made Syrah would be to get a bottle of Crozes Hermitage from that impeccable North Rhône producer Paul Jaboulet Ainé. Any Jaboulet wine is textbook stuff and the UK importers are O. W. Loeb of London SW1, though you can find the wines widely stocked elsewhere. Notice how intense the colour and flavour are. The tannin is marked but combined with a flavour quite unlike Cabernet Sauvignon. There's nothing here that would remind you of blackcurrants. The nearest fruit would be mulberries perhaps, but it's surely more mineral than vegetable (only Pinot is animal!). You could probably find a Syrah de l'Ardèche even cheaper. Made often from vines too young for a grander 'appellation', this will be thinner and without the rich fruit of a full-blooded Syrah.

The Syrah is also grown in the southern part of the Rhône Valley and by quality-conscious producers throughout the vast acreage of vineyards in southern France, 'the Midi'. It is very much a 'noble' grape, being designed for a long life and able to add firmness and an

Good examples of South Rhône wines helped by Syrah are superior Côtes-du-Rhône reds such as Lay & Wheeler's St Vincent and Château de Grand Moulas, stocked by Adnams of Southwold, Tanners of Shrewsbury and Balls Bros of London. The Chantovent wines

intriguing spiciness to blends of other grape varieties. You can tell a Châteauneuf-du-Pape or Côtes-du-Rhône from the southern Rhône Valley that has been toughened up by the addition of Syrah. It will have the blackish tinge and a certain amount of astringency not commonly found in other grapes of the Rhône and Midi. The Syrah produces wines that desperately need food to accompany them, so hard can they be, and they should not be broached for as long as you can bear to wait. The 1961 Hermitage La Chapelle from Paul Jaboulet Ainé has years ahead of it still, and, because it was such an exceptional year, tastes disconcertingly like a great 1961 Claret.

from the Château and Domaine de Gourgazaud in Minervois show that it can be a good thing in Midi wines too. The Syrah qualifies as one of the varieties officially designated 'cepage ameliorateur' and certainly adds colour and depth of flavour to these wines.

Côte Rôtie is different from the rest of the north Rhône reds listed above in that the good producers, of which there are but a handful, add a little of the local white grape, Viognier, to give the wine more delicacy and scent. The Viognier is very difficult to grow and is hardly planted anywhere outside the Côte Rôtie *appellation* and two neighbouring all-white ones, Condrieu and Château Grillet. (Although Joseph Phelps of California, a great lover of Rhône wines, is trying to cultivate some in the Napa Valley.) It has an intriguingly musky peach or apricot smell, is vinified to produce medium dry wines with lots of body because it is cultivated so far south, and is one of the most haunting white grapes there is. If you catch a whiff of this scent in a red wine, it will almost certainly be Côte Rôtie.

Specimens of Viognier are difficult to find and expensive when you do. Yapp Bros of Mere stock a good range of wines made from both Syrah and Viognier, as well as offering more than half a dozen examples of Côte Rôtie. They list Château Grillet as well as Condrieu, of which Les Amis du Vin of London W12 have a good supply too. Condrieu is better value than Château Grillet, but both have the fascinating aroma of this rare grape. An A-level exercise if ever there was one, but you could try to find the Viognier aroma in the bouquet of a Côte Rôtie.

Rhône wines are currently very good value, and unlike Burgundy to the north the Rhône Valley has experienced very few disappointing vintages recently. It is strange that the Syrah grape is not cultivated more widely when it's capable of producing such thrilling, long-lived wines.

Rhône vintages

1982–1981 Luscious and early maturing because slightly low in acidity.
1980 Rich with lots of fruit.
1979 Quite a bit of tannin and not as 'classic' as 1978.
1978 Stupendous.
1977 Much better than the rest of France; not thin.
1976 Full, sometimes fat.
1975 and 1974 Variable and not as luscious as some.

Older than this, you have to go back to 1968 to find a less than exciting vintage.

Even more bizarre is that the only country which does claim to grow a great deal of the grape, makes wines so unlike the greats of the north Rhône. The Shiraz, supposedly the same as the Syrah, is Australia's most widely planted wine grape and produces a great range of sweetish wines that are often brownish-red with no great intensity of anything – quite different from Hermitage. You may well find it difficult to see the connection between these two grapes. Nevertheless, some of Australia's Shiraz is great value at the moment, for they still have a glut of red grapes and no shortage of sunshine to ripen them. Try to memorize the hot, baked flavour of the typical Australian Shiraz. Those from the Hunter in New South Wales have my volcanic twang (others even describe the flavour as 'sweaty saddle'), while some of the richer ones from South Australia and Victoria can have a chocolatey flavour to them. They are all relatively sweet (even if labelled 'dry red') and high in alcohol. There is

Averys of Bristol and W. H. Cullen are good sources of Australian wines, of which Shiraz (often pronounced 'shir-ah') is probably the best value. Notice the obvious warmth in the flavour. These are wines made with a lot more sunshine than even the annual average in the Rhône Valley. Take note of the provenance of your Australian Shiraz, for Australia can't be regarded as a single wine region – it's about as big as Europe, after all.

often a lot of flavour to begin with but it can fall off leaving a thin, watery finish. Blends of Shiraz and Cabernet are quite common and often attractive because the Cabernet fills in the hollow of taste at the end.

In California, only Rhônophile Joseph Phelps and Estrella River offer much Syrah as a serious varietal, but there are extensive plantings of a grape they call Petite Sirah and which they thought for ages was a clone of Syrah. It seems more likely to be the descendant of a lesser and more obscure Rhône grape, but some winemakers there are quite enthusiastic about it. Petite Sirah has lots of tannin but a much coarser flavour than Syrah. It can be useful in blends to bone up the much less tannic Zinfandel. In sum, there's nothing petite about Petite Sirah.

Petite Sirah is bottled in California as a varietal, but a few examples find their way to this country, often for good reason. Wente's specimen is well under £4 and very full bodied. You should notice a definite colour correlation between this and the Rhône's Syrah. Much more interesting, and a worthy American cousin to good Hermitage, is Joseph Phelps' Syrah, available from Les Amis du Vin.

Grenache and other rosés

While some of the beefier Châteauneuf-du-Papes and other southern Rhône wines may contain a bit of Syrah, Grenache is the most commonly planted grape there. It is distinguished by an unusual combination of paleness of colour and high alcohol, and has a sweet, fruity flavour that is a bit like a very strong mixture of Beaujolais and a good Pinot Noir – but with a bit of herbiness. It is widely grown in Provence and seems to pick up a bit of that that region's lovely scent of lavender and wild thyme. (If you think this must be complete fancy on my part, try Heitz Martha's Vineyard Cabernet and note how it picks up the eucalyptus flavour of

Les Amis du Vin of London W12 may just be able to supply an example of the famous and expensive Martha's Vineyard.

the trees round about that patch of vines.)

Most Châteauneuf and other south Rhône wines are made from a mixture of grapes and it can be interesting to taste them knowing this. See if you can notice that they, like another blend, Rioja, taste more soupy – more like a mixture of different flavours than one dominant one. There are properties, however, that specialize in making a wine from Grenache only. This provides a good opportunity to come to grips with the flavour of this grape, which – as Garnacha – is an important ingredient in the typical red Rioja blend.

Each time you taste a Châteauneuf-du-Pape, try to assess how much Syrah it contains. If you don't taste much Syrah, then the predominant grape variety is probably Grenache. The average Châteauneuf contains about 10 per cent Syrah, 65 per cent Grenache and a mixture of other local grape varieties, though some Châteuneufs are made without any Syrah at all, and the wonderfully complex Château Rayas (available from O. W. Loeb of London SW1) is made from nothing but Grenache. It has a deep colour from long fermentation and exceptionally low yields, but does have the ripe spiciness of which this grape is capable. Notice how sweet Grenache is.

Because of its light colour, Grenache is in great demand as chief ingredient for pink wine and predominates in the taste of the powerful rosés of Tavel and Lirac. Notice the high alcohol content, pale colour and a certain lusciousness, even if the wine is basically dry. Most rosés are made in the same way as red wines, except that the must is run off the skins after a much shorter time so that much less colouring matter is absorbed. A few wines are made pink by fermenting red and white grapes together on the skins. Some cheap rosés are made by simply blending together red and white wines, but their flavour is likely to be fairly unharmonious as the ingredients can bear little relation to each other, and won't be given time to 'marry'. Any blending in winemaking should be followed by at least one year's settling time and preferably more,

Any Tavel or Lirac and most Provence rosés will demonstrate the Grenache as a rosé. Notice that a rosé can be quite as full bodied as a red wine, and have just as much acidity as a white. See if you can smell Provençal herbs in these wines.

Contrast these 'proper' rosés with a cheap blended one – anything at the bottom end of the price range will do (so, I'm afraid, may the famous brands). See if you can tell whether the wine was a late-stage blend.

Take a glass of any two whites and make full note of their flavours and attributes. Blend them together in a third glass and compare the result. It won't be nearly as exciting. The blending process seems to result in the lowest common denominator of

but that is a luxury that the blenders of inexpensive table wine can ill afford. You can see for yourself that if you blend two wines the result tastes much duller initially than the sum of the components.

Rosés are not generally thought of as 'serious' wines. All the more reason to get lots of fun out of them by establishing which style you like: dry and herby as in Provence rosés or slightly sweet and herbaceous as in Cabernet d'Anjou, the superior neighbour of Rosé d'Anjou that doesn't actually have to have Cabernet in it.

each wine. Contrast this with your memory of a fine Claret, for which the different vats were blended well before bottling and probably three or four years at least before you enjoyed the wine.

See if you can spot the Cabernet scent of a Cabernet d'Anjou. It can also taste a bit like a Sauvignon Blanc, nicely establishing the family link between that white grape and the Cabernet family.

Nebbiolo, the foggiest

Italophiles wake up. Your time has come at last. The great wines of Italy have not been mentioned so far because they tend to come from (red) grapes that are rarely encountered outside Italy. For years Italy was an island in terms of wine production and appreciation, though the 'classic' grapes of the rest of Europe have been gaining ground – quite literally – all over the country and especially in the north-east. These 'new' Cabernets, Pinots, Rieslings and Chardonnays apart, most of the grapes grown in Italy are foreign in name and taste to most non-Italians. Only the workhorse white variety Trebbiano, grown in quantity all over central Italy, is seen much elsewhere, and this is only as the rather undistinguished Ugni Blanc used as base wine for Cognac. The very high acidity level and low level of character are desirable for distillers, and can be useful for makers of white wine in climates as hot as many parts of Italy.

You will see how 50% more sunshine tastes

Italy's greatest wines come from pockets of cooler vineyards, usually by virtue of altitude, and its most famous fine wine region is Piedmont. Here the Nebbiolo grape is king, and the locals claim for their most famous wine (as others have done elsewhere) that Barolo is the 'king of wines and wine of kings'. Nebbiolo gets its name from the mist or *nebbia* that can shroud the vineyards in these Alpine foothills in the autumn, and is grown

Italian specialists include Cynthia Bacon of South Harting, Hants; Luigi's of Parson's Green; Millevini of Disley, Cheshire; Stonehaven Wines of Bordon, Hants; and Woods of Lindfield, West Sussex. The Market, Le Provençal, Harrods and Les Amis du Vin should also list some good examples. Names to look for among producers of Barolo and Barbaresco include Ceretto, Aldo Conterno, Fontanafredda, Franco-Fiorina, Gaja, Bruno Giacosa, Pio throughout the region to produce its longest-living wines. I find it easy to confuse Nebbiolo with Syrah, certainly in appearance and structure if not in flavour. The Nebbiolo is a very tannic grape that translates into very tannic, dark-coloured wines – though new techniques in the vineyard and cellar have tended to lighten the colour of wines made during the 1970s. The hallmark of Nebbiolo is its bouquet, one of those smells that have non-wine-drinkers screeching with incredulous mirth when they read the classic descriptions: violets, truffles and liquorice are all common terms of appreciation for this very dry, full-bodied tannic wine. There's usually more obvious fruit and scent in a good Nebbiolo than in most youthful Syrah-based wines, and I sometimes find the great Italian Piedmont grape tastes rather pruney.

Cesare, Alfredo Prunotto, Renato Ratti. Fontanafredda wines may be some of the easiest to find, being stocked by Peter Dominic among others, but are not the most exciting. Gaja's are the most unusual and least typical, some of them being very juicy indeed. Victoria Wine have stocked one of his Barbarescos. Notice how strong, dry and tannic the wines are, but try to get to grips with their amazingly intense scent. You may be able to find violets or even the local Alban truffles there – if you've been lucky enough to taste these delicacies.

A-level: Compare a Syrah-based wine with one made from Nebbiolo of about the same age and quality of vintage (see below). Notice that the Nebbiolo is slightly stronger, probably slightly bitter and with a more voluptuous smell.

The trouble with wines made from Nebbiolo is that, although they all come from this corner of north-west Italy, there can be enormous variation in quality and style. Barolo and its rather lighter neighbour Barbaresco are the most famous, but Boca, Caramino, Carema, Fara, Gattinara, Ghemme, Lessona, Sizzano, Spanna and wines labelled as Nebbiolo are all based on the grape. Barolo is fashioned to last the longest, but a good Barbaresco can be less of an assault on the senses. Most of these wines are very strong; Barolo must reach a natural strength of 13° at least.

If you can compare a Barolo and Barbaresco from the same producer you will see that the latter is lighter in colour and body. You can broach most Barbaresco after about five years, but have to wait for eight with many Barolos. It is difficult to find the other Nebbiolo wines here except for a few rather coarse Spannas and some interesting, approachable wines labelled simply Nebbiolo.

Traditionally winemakers in Barolo and Barbaresco would ferment the grapes on the stalks as well as with the skins for a protracted period, and

Producers who have made modifications to the traditional way of making Barolo and Barbaresco include: Ceretto (whose wines are

then keep them for years in large and ancient chestnut casks – sometimes until the sales order was received, so that a wine might spend twelve years in wood and no time in the bottle before being sold. This tended to make a wine that was naturally very tannic, even drier and leaner of fruit flavour. Only in exceptionally fruity years could the wine be drunk rather than chewed. Things are changing now, however. Many winemakers have bought new casks and stainless-steel vats in which to ferment and extract maximum fruit from the grapes (without the stalks to emphasize the astringency). The wines are now kept in cask for a much shorter period (though the DOC laws still insist on a minimum of two years – even in lean vintages), and producers purposely give them extended bottle age to soften them, before putting them on the market. You can taste an enormous difference in different styles of these wines.

often marketed under the individual vineyard name – surprisingly rare in Italy – such as Bricco Rocche and Bricco Asili), Franco-Fiorina, Gaja (whose wines are very juicy indeed), Alfredo Prunotto and Renato Ratti. Look out for their wines at any of the stockists mentioned above. Try to compare one of their recent vintages with a more traditionally made wine. Pio Cesare makes wines of great quality that have not been swayed by the wind of change in Piedmont. Some other producers have been responsible for some pretty nasty, tough wines. Notice how much more obvious the fruit is in the 'new' wines, and how much more noticeable the tannin is in the 'old' ones.

The gentle revolution in winemaking techniques makes recommending recent vintages a dangerous business, as the exact producer and their policy on 'modern' winemaking has a great influence on the likely taste of the wine. However, this is a general guide for Piedmont vintages of red wine.

Piedmont vintages

1981 Disappointing, not sufficient fruit.
1980 Could be good.
1979 Low in tannin and easy; early-drinking wines with charm.
1978 A classic, but not till the late 1980s.
1977 Mean.
1976 Some fruity wines for early consumption.
1975 Average.
1974 Very good, full-bodied wines for keeping.

The other recent great years were 1970 and 1971, many of which are just softening to become wonderful wines now.

Piedmont is also the home of two more definitely Italian grape varieties: Barbera and Dolcetto, not often enough available in Britain. Barbera produces dry, acid reds not unlike the red Vinho Verde wines of Portugal though medium bodied. These should usually be drunk young and slightly chilled, and with a completely different frame of mind than that required for the great Nebbiolo. Dolcetto is even more frivolous and gulpable though not sweet, despite the name. It is dry, very fruity and often rather inky. Its aroma has a certain smooth grapiness about it.

Sangiovese, by Jove

The other great red wine grape of Italy is the Sangiovese, named after Saint Jove. It is grown all over central Italy but is primarily responsible for Chianti. The Chianti laws are very strict as to exactly what proportions of different grapes are allowed into the blend, but Sangiovese always represents the major contribution, between 50 and 70 per cent by law but often more in practice. White grapes, including the unprepossessing Trebbiano, comprise most of the rest of the blend (unusually for a red wine) so that most Chianti is quite pale in colour.

Sangiovese is one of those grapes of which many different clones have been planted, with widely varying results. The best way initially to come to grips with 'typical' Sangiovese is to taste a well-made Chianti, probably a Chianti Classico that comes from the heartland of the Chianti region, and preferably a *riserva* that has had time to soften and show at its best. Much of the Sangiovese planted in Chianti is quite pale (though the Sangiovese Grosso described below is very deeply coloured) and ripens late. Other characteristics are marked acidity and a certain rustic flavour.

Any of the Italian specialists listed on page 138 should stock a good selection of Chiantis. It is important to make the distinction between simple DOC Chianti, with only the name of a big producer or bottler on the label, and the single estate wines which are usually put into Claret-shaped straight-sided bottles made of very dark brown glass (not the wicker flask which is an expensive bit of tourist folklore today). Chianti Classico is a reliable DOC, more stringent than Chianti, and each bottle has a seal showing a black cockerel on the capsule. One excellently made example, Antinori's Santa Cristina, is available from Victoria Wine. Choose your example with reference to the vintage notes below, and try to make up your own palate picture of the Sangiovese. Note the interesting bouquet and try to formulate your own trigger word for it. Register paleness, acidity and bitterness too.

My tasting notes for Chiantis are littered with the word 'farmyardy' – though I like them a lot. As with so many Italian reds, there is also often the suggestion of bitterness. The main distinguishing marks of a Sangiovese-based Chianti are therefore: pale red, going brownish after only three or four years; a smell of old vegetation (or old animals); lots of acidity; some bitterness and a certain coarseness of texture. Some youthful Chiantis may feel very slightly sparkling. This is because they have been made with the traditional *governo*, the addition of dried grape must to re-ferment in the wine after the initial alcoholic fermentation.

Guessing the vintage is only significant for wines that develop interesting characteristics with age

As it ages, the wine gets paler and more brown in colour and, I think, reaches a peak at about five to eight years. After this the wines start to dry out as the initial fruitiness of a Chianti blend, containing as it does some rather neutral-flavoured white grapes, is not high.

Tuscany vintages

1981 Concentrated and good.
1980 Not a success.
1979 Very forward, fruity and useful though it may not keep well.
1978 Excellent; lots of everything.
1977 Good for both Chianti and Brunello.
1976 Hardly seen.
1975 Good quality and lots of fruit.
1974 Poor and lean.

Other recent good vintages were 1970 and 1971. For relevant details of now-drinkable vintages of Brunello di Montalcino, first consult your bank manager.

Sangiovese is grown all over Romagna and Umbria as well as Tuscany. Its most ordinary manifestation widely available in this country is as poor quality Sangiovese di Romagna that should be drunk as young as possible. It reaches its most famous and expensive peak in Brunello di Montalcino, made

A good quality assessment exercise would be to try to distinguish blind between an inexpensive Sangiovese di Romagna and a fairly young Chianti Classico. There should be much more flavour in the more expensive wine to illustrate what the cheaper one lacks.

exclusively from a strain of Sangiovese Grosso and probably Italy's (the world's?) longest-living wine. The firm of Biondi Santi has done much to boost the price and reputation of these wines, and they are unpalatably tannic and concentrated when young. Biondi Santi's Il Greppo *vino da tavola* is lighter and made of younger vines.

You will usually have to go to an Italian specialist for Brunello, and the wines of Biondi Santi – which represent the pinnacle of Brunellosity – are very difficult to find. If you do manage to taste the wine (and I don't recommend it as good-value drinking) you will notice an enormous amount of colour and tannin. The wine is very dry but, if you can find it, it should have lots of fruit in there lurking behind the tannin, waiting for it to move off. Alivini of London EC1 import Il Greppo – a less expensive way to try embryonic Brunello.

In the Chianti region there has been a similar sort of revolution to that in Piedmont. Some of the more progressive producers have been fighting for a reduction in the amount of white wine officially required in the blend, and some of them have been quietly omitting the Trebbiano (that was only ever written into the laws because there was a surplus of it and it is particularly easy to grow). Some have even been experimenting with small oak cooperage as in Bordeaux, an alternative to the much bigger Slovenian oak casks traditionally used. This tends to produce much more elegant wines capable of longer life and well suited to subsequent bottle-ageing. Antinori have been pioneers of this and their Tignanello represents the effects of small oak, no white grapes and the addition of up to 10 per cent Cabernet Sauvignon to the traditional Chianti blend. It's a fascinating example of the power this Bordeaux grape has to shape flavour even in small quantities. Also in Tuscany, the 250-year-old tradition of adding up to 10

Most of the Italian stockists listed on page 138 should have one vintage of Tignanello, as do many other specialist wine shops and even the biggest off-licence chain in Britain, Victoria Wine. This is a delicious well balanced wine that you should try to compare with a well-made Chianti Classico. Notice the much deeper, more blueish colour of the Tignanello and how even a small amount of Cabernet is apparent on the nose. You may also find the flavour of oak and, if the wine is young, the tannin will be more pronounced on the Tignanello. Tignanello 1978, for instance, is a great, concentrated wine built to last for twenty years.

per cent Cabernet to the Carmignano blend demonstrates that this has made sense for years.

Stonehaven Wines of Bordon, Hants, and Windrush Wines of Cirencester, Glos, should have a Carmignano in stock. Those of the Villa di Capezzana are particularly good and taste slightly more traditionally Italian than Tignanello.

Another example of Cabernet's more recent invasion of Italy (and also under the Antinori auspices) is Sassicaia, grown on the Tuscan coast from 100 per cent Cabernet Sauvignon and given similar cellar treatment to Tignanello. This wine shows that Italy is eminently capable of producing delicious wines from imported grapes, though you will probably find it easy to distinguish it from a Claret.

Try the Italian specialists again for Sassicaia. Remember this is all Cabernet and try to relate it to other Cabernets you have tasted. A comparison of Sassicaia with a Claret of the same age and price and a California Cabernet in the same range would be fascinating. The Sassicaia may well taste more like the American than its fellow European, for the micro-climate at the Tenuta San Guido, just south of Livorno, is hotter than the Médoc – much more like sunny California.

5 Further tasting

More white grapes

Aligoté: the 'other' white grape of Burgundy and not nearly as noble as Chardonnay. Light, very tart, pale and not capable of long life. Best from Bouzeron.

Most Burgundy shippers offer a Bourgogne Aligoté. They taste best from ripe vintages, and Adnams of Southwold have one of the best.

Alvarinho: the best grape that goes into white Vinho Verde, and grown as Albariño just over the Spanish border in Galicia. Is fragrance can be almost Viognier-like in its rich peachiness, even though the wines are very high in acidity and usually vinified very dry.

Palaçio de Brejoeira is 'the' Vinho Verde and an Alvarinho wine, though most Vinho Verde should have a little bit of the perfume. Hurlingham Wines should stock it. Laymont & Shaw of Truro have a delicious Castel do Fornos made in Galicia from Albariño.

Chasselas: unusually, a wine grape that is also found in the fruit basket. It's responsible for common table wines in the middle Loire and, as Elbling, for almost all of the light, dry and acid wines of Luxembourg and for the most ordinary wines of the Mosel. In Switzerland it is called Dorin or Fendant, and occasionally takes on an attractive light smoky character.

Any wine called simply Pouilly-sur-Loire will be Chasselas (as opposed to the Sauvignon-based Pouilly-Fumé). Luxembourg wines are rarely exported, but London's Swiss Centre has a good stock of Swiss wines.

Furmint: Hungary's slightly spicy white grape that usually produces dry wines with a certain amount of body. Makes the wonder-wine Tokay, with the even more obscure Hárslevelü.

Most good wine shops have Tokay in various forms – the most basic Tokay Furmint, Tokay Szamorodni, or the rich and gold, almost sherry-like Tokay Aszu which comes in increasing 'puttonyos', or degrees of sweetness (five is the richest).

Gros Plant: the less fruity grape of the Muscadet region, it is

I wouldn't search too hard for Gros Plant.

responsible for wines with marked acidity and very little charm; though it must be said that they are refreshing.

Grüner Veltliner: Austria's native grape with a lovely racy spiciness to it. Wines usually have this aroma with at least medium body, but enough acidity to keep them well balanced.

Austrian specialists include the West End Wine Centre of London W1, but the branded wine Schluck should give you some idea of the attractive fruitiness of the grape.

Muscadet: the name of the grape and the wine, produced at the mouth of the Loire around Nantes. Very crisp and fairly neutral in character, though exceptional vintages produce fruity wines which can mature. Otherwise, it is to be drunk young as an uncomplicated lubricant.

There can be few wine shops, and even fewer restaurants and wine bars, where at least one Muscadet is not stocked. Perhaps it's so popular precisely because it's so bland; and its dryness and acidity feel clean, as though they are doing you good. Lorne House Vintners of Cranleigh specialize in mature Muscadet.

Pinot Gris: a grape of many names – Tokay in Alsace, where it can make almost Burgundian full-bodied dry whites; Ruländer in Germany and Austria, where it makes 'bigger' wines than usually encountered in either of those countries; Pinot Grigio in north-east Italy, where its wines are crisp and dry but with a slight hint of smoky fragrance.

The grape produces excellent well-balanced wines in Alsace, where the name Pinot Gris is taking over from Tokay (nothing to do with the great Hungarian wine of the same name). An Alsace Pinot Gris and an Italian Pinot Grigio should not be too difficult to find.

Seyval Blanc: a popular hybrid (between the European wine-producing vine *vitis vinifera* and wild native vines) grown in England to produce clean, dry whites with a certain suggestion of German *trocken* about them.

Most English wines state the main grape variety on the label. Spots Farm of Tenterden in Kent have produced particularly toothsome examples – the combination of cleanliness and fruitiness can be quite hard to track down. The Vintner's Wain of London SW1 and the English Wine Centre of Alfriston are good places to buy British.

Viura: the white grape of Rioja, though I've found it difficult to isolate its characteristics. New-style

Any white Rioja will do, but I have found the Solar de Samaniego Blanco, imported by Arriba Kettle of

white Rioja seems denuded of flavour, and traditional stuff tastes mainly of oak and age.

Birmingham and listed by Laymont & Shaw of Truro, to be an especially good demonstration of the floweriness of the Viura's bouquet. CUNE now produce a 'Vivra Blanco'.

More red grapes

Aramon: widely planted throughout the Midi, where it produces oceans of cheap, thin, unexciting wine. This high-yielder is one of the main causes of the European wine lake. The authorities are trying to encourage its grubbing up and the replanting of superior varieties.

Any cheap red 'vin de table' will probably demonstrate the rather inky, dank flavour of the Aramon grape. There's something faintly reminiscent of foxgloves about it.

Carignan: called Carignane in California, it is also grown throughout the Midi, where crossed with Cabernet Sauvignon it is responsible for the vibrant juicy Ruby Cabernet. Another Midi staple grape, as well as being found in the southern Rhône and many other hot wine regions around the world, where it produces alcoholic wines with lots of colour but little subtlety.

Carignane varietals are available from California and many inexpensive California reds may contain more than a dash of the grape. It's another major ingredient in southern French reds, or try to sift the Garnacha out of Tres Torres. Cariñena is what's left.

Cinsau(l)t: another southern Rhône grape, but with an attractive spicy character added to its colour and alcohol.

Lebanon's Château Musar wines provide a good example of the influence of Cinsaut (and lots of sunshine) on Cabernet-based wine.

Kadarka: fiery red grape grown throughout Austria, Yugoslavia and – particularly – Hungary, where it was principal flavour-shaper of Bull's Blood.

Most Hungarian reds contain a fair bit of Kadarka, and the famous Bull's Blood contains some still.

Tempranillo: you will rarely have the chance to taste this grape unblended, but it is the principal ingredient in

Torres Coronas from Penedes is chiefly Ull de Llebre and shows, in comparison with their Tres Torres

the typical red Rioja blend. It is also found, as Ull de Llebre, in the Penedes. I have found a flavour of tobacco about this grape, inasmuch as I have been able to isolate it.

blend of Garnacha and Cariñena, how much higher in acidity and how much paler and more 'serious' this grape is. Most red Riojas will demonstrate the same thing.

Zinfandel: a very important grape in California and capable of being vinified into all sorts of different styles of wine, from jammy Beaujolais-like to intense and rigorous long-life Pomerol-like. Its distinguishing mark is a smell of hot berries and a deep colour. It may be related to the much less common Primitivo grape of southern Italy.

There should be no shortage of 'Zins'. Christian Brothers have always made one that is very well balanced halfway between the two extremes of style, and this wine should be available from Peter Dominic. Ridge take Zinfandel more seriously than most, and their wines, available from Les Amis du Vin of W12 and others, demonstrate how noble the grape can be if given the Bordeaux treatment of small oak ageing. The Wine Studio of SW1 and La Vigneronne of SW7 should carry a wide range of California wines.

Wines without great grape genealogy

There are wines whose flavour is not fashioned by one predominant grape variety. Red Rioja is one of these and has already been examined in the section on red wine and oak. Châteauneuf-du-Pape also usually contains a mixture of grapes, though Grenache usually predominates. Most Portuguese reds, and the most famous Dão in particular, are made up of a mixture of grape varieties, with Tourigo, not encountered elsewhere, the most important. Dão can often be distinguished by its high glycerine content, which makes it very viscous, and a sublimation of pure fruit to quite a high tannin content which can give a rather astringent end-taste. Dão is deep in colour and in some cases needs about ten years to soften.

Adega Wines of Bristol and A. O. L. Grilli of Staplehurst, Kent, specialize in Portuguese wines, and Oddbins have traditionally carried a wider range than most. Try other Portuguese reds too and you will probably note similar characteristics.

Perhaps the most obvious example of a wine style which is recognizable by some characteristic other than grape variety is Retsina, the resinated family of Greek wines. They smell of pine or floor polish, depending on whether they're drunk in a beach taverna or in the bleak British midwinter, and you should need little guidance to recognize them.

Camden Town and the Greek Islands, in reverse order, are the best hunting grounds for Retsina.

The cheap table wines and famous brands are rarely based on a single grape variety. Doubtless there is plenty of Aramon in most red *vin de table* (as well as a hefty dollop of Italian *vino da tavola* to give it colour), and in various parts of the world the good old Sultana is responsible for gallons of white table wine. The best known brands which exhibit varietal characteristics are summarized here, and can be a good first step in learning.

Bull's Blood – Mainly Gamay.
Branded claret – Mainly Cabernet Sauvignon and Merlot; famous names include Mouton Cadet, Harveys No. 1 and La Cour Pavillon.
Hirondelle – Most are mixes of grapes, but their Bulgarian Cabernet Sauvignon provides an inexpensive way of sampling this noble variety.
Laski Riesling – The less noble Italian or Welsch Riesling, usually branded Lutomer, Cloberg or Pecs.
Liebfraumilch – There are hundreds of brands of this commonplace German blend, which usually demonstrates only very loosely the Müller-Thurgau type plus a dollop of a new aromatic variety; Blue Nun, Black Tower and Crown of Crowns are some of the most popular.
Mateus Rosé – If you can detect any positive character in this wine, you're a better taster than me.
Piat – The red Beaujolais is a good start-off for tasting Gamay, and the white Mâcon-Viré could provide a first sampling of Chardonnay.
Schluck – Austria's Grüner Veltliner.

More A-level exercises

Grafted *v.* ungrafted

In the second half of the nineteenth century the vineyards of Europe were devastated by a little bug, the *phylloxera vastatrix* (vastatrix indeed!) which, having been imported by accident from America, munched its way through the roots of European *vitis vinifera* vines. All sorts of solutions were sought, and in the end the only effective one was found to be grafting *vitis vinifera* cuttings on to rootstock of wild native American vines that had developed a resistance to *phylloxera*. To this day, about 90 per cent of the world's vineyards are planted with these 'grafted' vines. There are little pockets of land where vines are 'ungrafted', either because there seems to be no danger of *phylloxera* striking (the louse hates sand) or because, by chance, it has never struck (as in Bollinger's tiny Vieilles Vignes patch in Champagne). You can taste the difference between the wines produced by these ungrafted vines and the rest. The flavour seems much more positive and full blown, sometimes almost pushily so. Here are some examples of ungrafted wines that you can afford. Next time you drink an early nineteenth-century wine, though, bear in mind that it too would have been produced from pre-phylloxera vines.

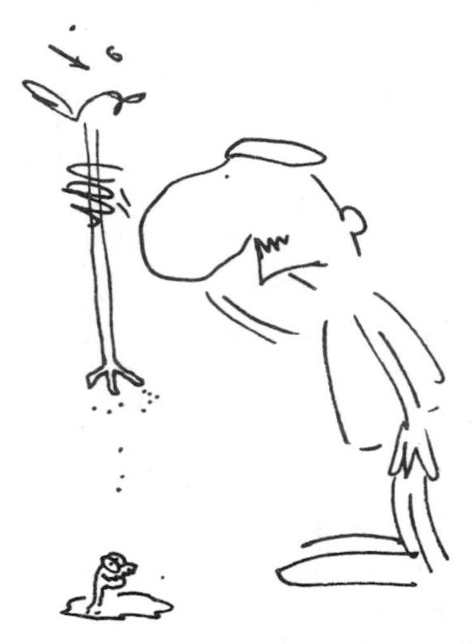

Ungrafted territory:

All of Chile (taste how ripely fruity Chilean Cabernets are).
Much of South Australia and New South Wales.
Monterey County in California.
Washington State and much of Oregon.
Much of the Mittelrhein in Germany.
Round the Neuseidlersee in Austria (Rust, Apetlon, etc.).
Colares near Lisbon.
Listel and SICAREX wines from the sandy shores of the Mediterranean.

Age of the vine

The state of maturity of the individual vine plays an important part in determining the flavour of the

Two estates in the southern Médoc provide good examples of what a difference new plantings can make.

wine it produces. In quantitative terms the vine starts producing a sensible amount of wine in its third year and reaches a peak at about fifteen to twenty years, decreasing steadily so that at fifty years it is scarcely economic to cultivate such an aged plant. The quality of the wine produced steadily increases with age, however, so that really dedicated winemakers search out very old vines, however uneconomic their crop, to add depth and complexity of flavour to their blends. The older the vine, the deeper its roots and the wider the range of elements it can give to the wine. Wines from newly planted vineyards can taste rather thin and simple, while those from ancient vines have many more layers of flavour. You can seek out new plantings and old plantings, such as those suggested here, and compare the differences in character.

Château La Lagune was a run-down property in 1958, when bought and revitalized by extensive new plantings. Its early 1960s vintages, while good, probably contained a lot of young-vine wine, which slowly mellowed and deepened throughout the decade. Its neighbour Château Cantemerle was bought in 1980 and new plantings have already begun as part of a ten-year programme to extend the vineyard by about 200 per cent. New vintages of Cantemerle may demonstrate the young-vine character too, though Bordeaux châteaux often sell off the produce of their younger vines rather than alter the character of the 'grand vin' that carries the château name.

Perhaps better examples are the wines of the Hautes Côtes of Burgundy where vines were planted in the late 1970s and the wines coming from there (in which Geisweiler specialize) are still a little thin in flavour. Look too at Chardonnays coming from anywhere in the world that does not have a Chardonnay-growing tradition. Italy and Spain provide particularly good examples.

Different vineyard sites

In a sense, all fine wine tasting proves the extraordinary point that different vineyard sites, even adjacent ones, produce wines of quite different character. To demonstrate (though not necessarily explain) the phenomenon to yourself, taste any selection of Clarets chosen using Hugh Johnson's invaluable *World Atlas of Wine* (Mitchell Beazley) as a guide, or any set of wines from the Rhine and Mosel. The lesson is

O. W. Loeb of London SW1 should be able to provide some excellent German examples of the nearby vineyards, encapsulated in affordable bottles by the same producer of the same vintage. Or you could try the experiment with different Grand Cru Chablis. O. W. Loeb, again, usually stock a wide range of the different 'grand cru' vineyards of the top quality Chablis producer Louis Michel.

particularly apt if the wines have both winemaker and vintage in common. I can think of no better example than a range of wines from the great Mosel winemaker J. J. Prüm. His adjacent Wehlener Sonnenuhr and Graacher Himmelreich clearly show how much more sunshine the former attracts simply because it's oriented a few more degrees towards the sun on the banks of the river.

You could of course stray into the minefield of the Côte d'Or, but there are so many variables here, I think you'd better play safer and cheaper elsewhere.

Low-temperature fermentation

There are certain cellar techniques which leave a very strong stamp on the character of the resultant wines. Carbonic maceration is one that we have studied already in its effects on red wines. Low-temperature fermentation has had the strongest impact on white wines made today. The principle is that by controlling the fermentation and making it happen very slowly at low temperatures, you keep everything very clean, pure and fresh. (For fine wines you're also in danger of failing to make an interesting enough cocktail of the potential flavours, but that's another story.) Some of the less expensive examples of this technique shriek 'modern winemaking' at me, much more loudly than they do their origins. Here are some examples of such wines. Look for their purity of flavour, high acidity and a characteristic that is almost steely but perhaps just very slightly dull.

'Modern' dry white Riojas such as Marques de Caceres, Viña Leonora, Solar de Samaniego, and indeed nowadays almost all white Rioja apart from Marques de Murrieta and Tondonia from Lopez de Heredia.

Viña Sol and most dry white Torres wines.

The varietals of Friuli in north-east Italy, especially Pinots Bianco and Grigio.

Many other Italian dry whites, including Victoria Wine's Bianco di Custoza.

Listel dry whites.

Many South African, Australian and New Zealand whites; Brown Bros in the State of Victoria sometimes ferment their whites for weeks on end.

Bottle size

Wines kept in different sizes of bottle are thought to mature at different rates. Half-bottles encourage the wine to mature rapidly, perhaps without picking up quite such interest along the way as a standard bottle size or, reckoned to be most satisfactory of all, the magnum (containing 1.5 litres or two standard bottles). This is why a magnum of fine wine usually costs more than two standard bottles. Bottles even bigger are often sold more for their novelty value. They terrify me. Just think of dropping a jeroboam of Château Lafite.

Compare the development of a fairly mature and (I'm afraid) fairly grand wine in different bottle sizes. Cheap wine isn't made to develop anyway, so there's no point in monitoring progress; it will always be downhill.

6 Wine, food and fun

Wine and food are not a suitable subject for a book. All the relevant guidelines can be given in a short chapter such as this, or it demands a lifetime of research and dissatisfaction. If you are a purist, you could probably – after many disappointments – find the single wine that would best accompany each food or dish you allowed past your lips. You might match a hearty beef stew, for instance, with Châteauneuf-du-Pape because it too is made up of a maceration of different flavour components. If the stew were to be served with carrots you might choose a wine that depended heavily on the Grenache grape, to complement the sweetness in that vegetable. And if the accompanying potatoes were little new ones, you might be swayed towards a Châteauneuf of recent vintage, while older baked potatoes would suggest a more mature example. See what I mean? You can let the business of matching solids and liquids get out of hand. In general terms, you can enjoy almost any wine with almost any food.

Whatever you like your general approach will be to ram as much into your system as possible

This is particularly true since, in practice, we tend to enjoy food and drink at discrete intervals. We rarely find ourselves with a mouth of food and wine mixed up together – only if we're feeling particularly greedy. What usually happens is that we consume what's in front of us, or rather we take a selection of the food

Next time you're having wine with a meal, notice how you consume the solid and the liquid constituents. You'll probably find that you take a mouthful of the wine before you actually eat anything, which is a very good moment at which to taste it as consciously as possible. Thereafter you use the wine as lubricant for the on our plate and then, when we're feeling thirsty, a mouthful of wine. So long as what we've just eaten doesn't completely destroy our tasting faculties, we can enjoy almost any wine, whatever its character.

solid matter you are taking in – just as you would use a glass of water in fact.

In Chapter 2 substances that distracted from the business of wine tasting were discussed, and there are a few specific foods that might be served at a meal which would make it more difficult for you to appreciate wine. This is not to say you should never again eat chocolate or mint sauce, simply that it is unwise to serve your guests a very special bottle of wine when at the same time asking them to rinse their mouths with such distracting flavours.

Try to monitor what effect the food you eat has on the taste of the wine you're drinking. Compare the sensations given you by that first mouthful savoured before you tasted the food and the mouthful of wine immediately after your first eating session.

Acids: anything *very* high in acidity makes wine a bit difficult to taste afterwards, or at least usually makes the wine taste more acid (which means of course that a flabby wine, such as a full-bodied North African or southern Spanish number, might well taste better when interpersed with mouthfuls of sharply dressed salad). 'Buy on an apple and sell on cheese' is an old wine-trade adage, illustrating the flattering nature of cheese – it softens the palate and makes it ready for a gulp of wine – and the much less flattering effects of the acidity in apples on wine tasted immediately afterwards. Some acids seem kinder on wine than others. A squeeze of lemon juice isn't going to ruin a wine, but a vinaigrette too high in *vinaigre* is no fun for any wine – or for any palate for that matter.

Take some wine that you don't value too highly – or preferably two of very different styles, one light-bodied white and one full-bodied red. Now try the wines before and after mouthfuls of the following, all high in different sorts of acidity:

lemon juice (citric);
vinegar (acetic);
natural yogurt (lactic).

Try to monitor how much each affects the flavour of the wine, making sure that you get all of your mouth well rinsed in each substance. Notice how much more acid the wine tastes after the vinegar, though less markedly so after the lemon juice and yogurt. Might this suggest a modification to your salad dressings when serving wine? Notice too that the lighter-bodied wine is more affected. Strong-flavoured, full-bodied wines don't seem to mind the acid distractions too much.

Now try the apple and cheese trick. See how different a wine tastes after each – especially a young wine, the sort that was most frequently bought and sold and therefore gave rise to the adage.

Artichoke: globe artichokes have a strange metallic taste that makes any wine taste metallic too. Don't ask me to explain this, but don't waste great wine on the magnificent globe. It's got so much liquid in it that you probably won't want any lubrication anyway.

Next time you're eating artichoke or asparagus, try out this surprising theory about wine taken with them. Don't you find your mouth left with a distinctly un-winey flavour if you try to drink wine just after a mouthful of either vegetable?

Asparagus: almost the same applies as for globe artichokes.

Egg yolk: a soft yolk seems to coat the mouth and leaves your taste buds defenceless and dulled. But then how often do you have wine for breakfast?

Egg yolks are probably the least serious offenders in keeping you from wine-inspired pleasure. Nevertheless, try a glass of red wine with your next soft-boiled egg and notice how difficult it is to taste the wine properly.

Chocolate: very similar effect to soft yolks – again because of its texture. However, a lightly chocolate-flavoured mousse would not play havoc with your palate.

Ditto chocolate. Can you really judge a mouthful of wine after one of Dairy Milk? Incidentally, few of these tricky foods impair your smelling or 'nosing' abilities. You can still get most of the flavour of the wine, but you can't judge aspects such as sweetness, acidity and tannin properly, for which the inside of your mouth needs to be in prime unsullied tasting condition.

Kippers: they're very oily and salty. I suspect it's the oiliness that prevents you from properly savouring a wine, for much the same reason as egg yolks and chocolate are barred from the company of fine-for-wine foods. These and other very oily foods seem best countered with a very tannic wine.

Tea and kippers are made for each other. Prove it by trying them with wine instead of tea.

Mint: just as peppermints are not the best preparation for a wine tasting, very minty puddings or salads and (especially) a mint sauce that combines mint with vinegar are pretty poor accompaniment to fine wine.

Bendicks Bittermints and After Eights are double-killers of wine, of course. Don't try them till you know you don't want any more wine – though a very rich Port would probably get through the menthol and smear of cocoa butter.

Spices: subtly spiced dishes can be lovely partners for fairly full-bodied wines, but a vindaloo, it must be admitted, is not great with wine. Your mouth is left stinging and in no shape to measure the acidity, sweetness, etc, of a wine. You can still 'nose' a wine, but even your nasal passages are likely to have been heated up by the curry spices.

With curries, chilled beer can be deliciously refreshing – but if you really want to drink grape rather than grain, try the full-bodied, dry, but rather spicy wines of Alsace. You'll probably want something refreshingly cool, but it'll need lots of body weight to stand up to the spice.

There is a simple solution to the tricky problem of eating unsuitable food and enjoying wine at the same time. You can swiftly 'neutralize' your mouth after a mouthful of food by chewing something bland and absorbent such as bread, or simply swilling round a rinsing mouthful of water. A mouthful of bread after a sharply dressed salad or artichoke soon scrubs the mouth clean and ready for a taste of delicious wine.

After trying any of the 'danger' foods above, neutralize your mouth with either bread or water and see how much better you can taste the wine afterwards. However, curries and mint are too aromatic and affect the nasal passages as well, so they need more than bread and water – they need time – before you'll be on good wine-tasting form again.

There is one type of wine that is particularly useful for 'difficult' foods because it is full bodied, clean, dry but forceful enough to stand up to almost any solid. The driest Sherries, Fino and Manzanilla, are widely under-rated, and indeed underpriced. Because they are very good at stimulating the appetite, they're excellent first-course wines and would go happily with any salady dish, eggs, lots of spicy things and even the dread artichokes and asparagus. Fino with chocolate is not advised, however. Try milk.

Almost any wine shop has at least one Fino. Tio Pepe and La Ina are both very good, as can be La Guita Manzanilla, Tres Palmas and San Patricio. All Finos should be drunk as soon as possible after being bottled. Oddbins stocks particularly interesting Sherries.

So heretically relaxed am I about the business of wine and food that I don't even accept the rule that constitutes most people's knowledge of wine as a subject: white wine with fish and red wine with meat. I suspect what gave rise to it was the fact that most fish cries out for a bit of acidity to bring out its flavour – lemon juice, capers and even vinegar are standard accompaniments to fish – and white wines are usually higher in acidity than reds. In fact, this is only marginal. There are lots of red wines high in acidity that are delicious with fish, especially with fish that is stronger flavoured and relatively firm such as salmon, salmon trout, turbot, John Dory, sea bass, halibut and brill.

It is true that tannin, in which some red wines are high, does not go happily with delicate flavours of any sort and tends to leave a sort of inky taste. But light-bodied, low-tannin, high-acid reds such as those cited here would be fine with most fish dishes, especially those with a fairly rich sauce. These are wines you could serve coolish too if you want refreshment.

Serving temperatures of wine make a difference to how they taste, as we have seen, but the temperature at which you serve food is important too. Bear in mind that you won't be able to taste anything if you scorch or freeze your mouth. I may sound like an officious nanny, but don't expect to go wine tasting after a piping hot soup. Ice-cold sorbets are none too good either, I'm afraid, for they have a numbing effect on the inside of your mouth. Best to wait till you've finished eating a sorbet or

All these red wines should be fine with fish, especially fish that is full in flavour and robust in texture.

Almost any wine made by a version of 'macération carbonique' (and therefore low in tannin) such as Beaujolais, many Côtes-du-Rhône and juicy young Clarets such as Belair and Pierre Coste's.
Red Loire wines: Bourgueil, St Nicolas de Bourgueil, Chinon, Saumur-Champigny.
Most reds from Germany, Alsace or Austria.
South Tyrol (Alto Adige) reds.
Bardolino, Valpolicella, most light Italian Cabernets and some Chiantis, Barbera.
Red Burgundy from early-maturing vintages.
Most red 'vins de pays' from the South of France, Coteaux du Tricastin, Côtes de Ventoux, Côtes du Luberon.
Light 'clarete'-style Riojas in their youth.
Many New Zealand reds.

You could take equal enjoyment from any full-bodied white wine with many meat dishes. Again, it's body that matters more than colour.

You can chill wine by putting it in the deep freeze or ice box for twenty minutes

ice cream before attempting to taste wine, perhaps a very cold and not too-grand sweet white such as Monbazillac, 'country Sauternes'.

Much more important than temperature is the question of 'weight'. Even though you can enjoy all sorts of different flavours interleaved – a mouthful of poached halibut followed by one of youthful Claret can be lovely – mixing different weights of food and wine is usually a waste of the 'lighter' one. An avocado mousse is likely to be overwhelmed by a wine as strong as a Hermitage or Barolo, just as a delicate Mosel would be overpowered by the richness of jugged hare. With a subtly flavoured food it makes sense to serve a wine that's not too full bodied. With very strongly flavoured food, you would be foolish to expect a delicate wine to give much more pleasure than would a glass of water. Examples of wines that are particularly light and full bodied are given on page 30. Foods that are very 'full' and rich include anything that is highly spiced – which takes in curries and most dishes inspired by the Orient – very rich foods such as well-hung game and strongly sauced meats; strong cheeses, especially blue ones; rich meat pâtés, foie gras, mousses and terrines; and smoked fish, unless tempered with lots of bland cream and/or egg white.

With these guidelines, you will doubtless be able to come up with some delicious and exciting combinations of food and wine. If it's a casual family meal, then your choice of wine may be dictated by which bottle happens to be open –

These are some very enjoyable combinations of food and wine that you might not ordinarily think of.

Madeira with clear soup: a dry Madeira – Sercial or Verdelho – can be beautifully 'nutty' with a meat- or fish-based consommé or an even richer soup.

Foie gras and Sauternes: sounds disgusting, doesn't it? In fact, any rich livery mousse is delicious with an unctuous sweet wine (it must be full bodied, which rules out the Germans), provided there's lots of acidity.

Blue cheese and Sauternes: another strange-sounding combination that works very well, based on much the same principle of sweet and salty as ripe melon and Parma ham.

Cheese and wine are commonly accepted as ideal partners, being honoured to the extent of having a social function named after them. We naturally enough tend to think that French cheese will be an ideal match for French wine. But next time you have a ripe Camembert or Brie in the house, try it with a mouthful of wine and just see how the ammoniac quality in the cheeses wars with the flavour of the wine – making it taste bitter too. This does not apply to soft fat French cheeses in their youth, nor to the rather neutral Cantal, but certainly to many strong-flavoured French 'fromages' – not to mention 'formaggi' such in which case you might well learn all sorts of interesting things about unusual combinations of food and wine.

If you are trying to plan a selection of wines for formal entertaining, however, or simply to maximize informal enjoyment, it's worth bearing in mind the basics of choosing an order for wines: dry before sweet, light before full and young before old. Remember that four or more of you are likely to open at least a couple of bottles. It can be great fun, and very instructive, to serve two wines at the same time. This has the disadvantage of extra washing up, and possible accusations of pretension, but everyone will be surprised by how different two wines can seem when tasted together.

You can always take your lead for choice of wine from what's being cooked. With pasta you have a cast-iron excuse for an inexpensive Italian, or a better quality Chianti Classico Riserva. Paella suggests Rioja, red and/or white. Moussaka or kebabs allow you to introduce your friends to some of the better Greek wines such as Castel Danielis or Château Carras. None of these are expensive. And if you do feel duty bound, honour bound or perhaps promotion bound (when entertaining the boss) to spend a bit of money on wines for a special dinner, make sure you don't lash out on a wine that's not yet ready to drink. Trust in your nearest 'serious' wine merchant. You can judge how serious they are by the length of their replies to your questions, and they'll be delighted to advise on something more exciting than the price of the cheapest quarter-bottle of Scotch.

as Gorgonzola. England, so berated by most gastronomes, produces cheeses that are perfect partners for wine. Good farmhouse Cheddar is surely the most marvellous accompaniment to all but the most delicate wines. It is firm and offers no strong competition to the flavour of the wine, but still has its own character. Stilton is a bit more difficult. It can be so powerful, and so salty that, like Roquefort, it calls for something very sweet and strong. Port makes sense in the circumstance and proves that I'm not trying to be iconoclastic, merely sensible.

Always remember that, in matters of gastronomy, no matter how hard some people may aspire, there are no ultimate rules or arbiters. No one can point a finger at you and say, 'Thou hast sinned by serving me a Mâcon Blanc with Shepherd's Pie!' If you don't enjoy it, you've only yourself to blame, but your guests should be far too grateful that someone else is taking the trouble to give them a meal to criticize.

Glossary: some useful words for wine tasters

I hesitate to call this the definitive wine taster's vocabulary, for such a thing does not exist. The descriptive terms included here are just some of the words you'll find helpful to describe sensations caused by wine in *you*. Some, indeed most, of these words are quite commonly accepted. Others (marked *) are, quite frankly, humble but mine own. 'Blackcurrants' is, for instance, a far-from-unusual description of the Cabernet Sauvignon aroma, but I haven't heard anyone else call the ripe Chenin Blanc of the middle Loire 'gummy'.

Evolve your own vocabulary if it helps you, though a wide range of possible terms has been included here in the hope that specific flavours may lead you to specific grape varieties. Also included are some of the wine world's most abstruse bits of jargon, just so you can hold your own in vinous conversation.

acetic a wine gone *vinegary* by overexposure to air.

acid a wine described as 'acid' will have too much acidity.

acidity vital component in wine that gives 'bite' and life.

appellation name of the (usually French) wine. *Appellation contrôlée* wines are France's top ones, representing about 25 per cent of her production and usually named after the place they were made.

appley some young Chardonnays smell like this, though the smell of unripe apples signals an excess of malic acidity.

aroma that part of the smell of a wine that comes straight from the grapes (cf. *bouquet*).

aromatic very strongly perfumed, e.g. Sauvignon and Riesling grape varieties.

astringent the tactile sensation that an excess of tannin leaves on the insides of the mouth. Used especially for white wines (see *tannic*).

attenuated smart-sounding term for a wine that is drying out, i.e. losing fruit and charm because of age.

aura* my own word for the 'personal bouquet' surrounding the bodies of each of us.

baked a smell of heat and, usually, high alcohol. The flavour is often, but not necessarily, cooked out. Very hot grapes.

balance vital relative measuring of different elements in a wine, especially sweetness, *acidity*, fruit, tannin and alcohol. Any good mature wine should be well balanced, though a youthful one may still be 'out of balance'.

beefy* lots of body and quite a bit of tannin.

berries* warm berries is the giveaway smell of Zinfandel.

blackcurrants aroma of Cabernet Sauvignon, called *cassis* in French. The related Sauvignon Blanc can smell of blackcurrant leaves.

blowsy* a wine that has a lot of flavour at first, especially on the nose, but has no *length* and few indications (tannin if red and acid if white) that it will keep. Almost too much *fruit*.

body the measure of a wine's *weight*, a mixture of sugar, alcohol and extract.

boiled beetroot some people smell this on Pinot Noir.

botrytis cinerea a sort of rot that attacks grapes, shrivelling them and – if they're sweet and white – concentrating their lusciousness to good, and sometimes wonderful, effect. Red wines lose colour and are ruined if attacked by this mould, variously known as *noble rot, pourriture noble* and *Edelfäule*.

bouquet the smell in a wine that derives from its fermentation and, most importantly, maturation (cf. *aroma*).

burnt rubber* smell I associate with the Syrah grape.

breathe (v.i.) what a wine's supposed to do if you leave the bottle open for a bit before serving. This practice at least gives time for off-flavours to dissipate.

buttery the sort of richness (and colour) acquired by mature Chardonnay, traditionally associated with Meursault.

cachous* I find something of the scent of these pastilles on very aromatic grape varieties such as Gewürztraminer and Morio Muskat.

carbonic maceration way of making red wine by fermenting the uncrushed grapes. Tends to make full-flavoured, deep-coloured, low-tannin wines.

cardboard* my smell of stale materials that comes from poor treatment, often over-used filter pads.

cats' pee there's something of this in both Sauvignon Blanc and the intensely aromatic Scheurebe.

cedarwood traditional smell of a Claret given rigorous oak maturation; special characteristic of St Julien.

chaptalization commonplace (especially in France) practice of adding sugar to grape must in order to make the resultant wine stronger (though not sweeter).

château literally 'castle', but often the name for much less grand wine properties, especially in Bordeaux.

chewy very *astringent*.

chocolatey* a flavour I find in the often rather sweet reds of Australia and especially South Africa.

cigar box synonomous with *cedarwood*.

cigars some tasters smell cigars on Sémillon.

Claret what we British call the red wines of Bordeaux, often labelled Château Something.

classed growth one of the sixty or so châteaux arranged in 1855 into the top five classes from the Médoc and Graves, or included in subsequent classifications of Bordeaux properties. *Cru classé* in French.

clean no off-flavours.

clone particular group of vines produced from one cutting. Usually chosen in 'clonal selection', for one particular attribute such as high yield, disease resistance or even high quality.

cloying too sweet for the *acidity*.

coarse rough and ordinary without much interest.

commune French equivalent of a parish. Lots of wines are called after the commune in which they were made. A Gevrey-Chambertin is a commune wine, for instance.

complex lots of different well-married flavours that make a wine interesting, to the point of being fascinating.

concentrated lots of *fruit*, flavour and, often, colour too.

corked/corky wine with a definitely disgusting flavour, mouldy and rotten. Due to a poor cork usually, but even great tasting-gurus are not too clear about exactly how it happens. This is a flavour that's much more horrid than that of simple oxidation.

crisp a complimentary term for a white wine with refreshing *acidity*.

cru literally 'growth'. A *cru classé* is a classed growth, while a *grand cru* is a great growth.

cuvaison the extra period wine is left on the skins after fermentation to extract more from them.

damp straw* my trigger expression for Chenin Blanc, though many others prefer *honey and flowers*.

delicate rather airy-fairy term meaning light bodied and without very strong flavour, but well balanced.

dumb very little *nose*, common in youthful greats.

Edelfäule see *botrytis cinerea*.

eucalyptus cough linctus smell common in some concentrated California Cabernet Sauvignons.

farmyard* smell I associate with Chianti, especially aged Chianti, with some mature St Emilion and the odd rustically made Châteauneuf-du-Pape.

fermentation the vital process of turning grape juice into wine is the primary or alcoholic fermentation. The secondary fermentation, encouraged in cellars far from the Equator, is the malo-lactic fermentation that converts harsh malic acid into softer lactic acid.

figs another of those smells that other tasters associate with Sémillon.

finish important part of a wine's impact on the senses. What sort of impression it leaves at the end of the tasting process. A wine with a poor finish fades away to nothingness, and has no *length*.

firm not *flabby*, i.e. with sufficient *acidity*, and not in danger of falling apart because of age or acetic danger.

flabby too low in *acidity*.

flat dull and boring flavour often without enough *acidity*, or not sparkling if it's meant to be.

flinty confusing but oft-used term usually meaning *crisp* with a certain suggestion of cold stones. Sauvignon Blancs are often called 'flinty'.

flowery very fragrant in the way that flowers can be; floral scents.

forward a wine is described as forward if it tastes more mature than one would expect for its age.

fresh appealing because of its youth and *acidity*.

fruit very important component in the flavour of wines, especially young ones, deriving from the grapes themselves.

fruitcake* how the Merlot grape, especially in St Emilion, strikes me.

fruity wine with lots of appealing *fruit*.

full bodied wine with lots of *body*, as opposed to one that is medium bodied or *light*.

gamey wines that smell pungent in a ripe animal sense, such as a rich Syrah and Merlot (especially Pomerol).

geraniums unpleasant chemical smell, often associated with too much sorbic acid additive.

golden syrup* smell I associate with rich sweet whites, especially those affected by *botrytis*, and particularly Rieslings.

gooseberries 'green' sort of smell associated with Sauvignon Blanc.

governo technique still used in parts of Italy, especially Chianti, to add the prickle of a second fermentation to young wines by the addition of dried grape must to the wine after first fermentation.

grapey wine that smells of grapes, usually a Muscat.

green young wine with too much *acidity*.

gummy* the richness that very ripe Chenin Blanc grapes can bring to a wine.

gunshot* smell of rich mature Merlot, especially Pomerol. (Just one step ahead of *gamey*, after all.)

hard wine with too much tannin.

harmonious well balanced.

heavy too much alcohol and too little *acidity* for the fruit and sugar levels. According to EEC rules, heavy wines are those with an alcohol content of more than 15° (i.e. Sherry, Port and other fortified wines), as opposed to *light* wines.

herbaceous smell of grass and weeds, often found in the Cabernet family wines, especially Cabernet Franc.

herby* smell of thyme, lavender and pine sometimes found (perhaps fancifully) in the Grenache wines of Provence and the Midi.

hock German wines grown on the (sometimes outlying) banks of the Rhine. Wines from such regions come in tallish brown bottles as opposed to the green-bottled Mosel wines.

hollow wine with quite a bit of alcohol, but not much fruit to give a satisfying flavour and *weight* once in the mouth.

honey (and flowers) traditionally evocative tasting note for Chenin Blanc Loire wines and also for some German Rieslings.

inky red wine that tastes metallic, acid and often rather thin.

juicyfruit* luscious gulpable fruitiness, characteristic of Beaujolais.

lanolin rich, almost lemony flavour and texture taken on by good quality Sauternes.

length of flavour, a giveaway of quality in a wine. Any well-made wine that has had time to mature should leave a long aftertaste once it's been swallowed or expectorated. Such a wine 'finishes well'.

light the opposite of *full bodied* and not a pejorative term for wines that are meant to be delicate, such as many dry whites and some reds destined for youthful consumption. A light wine is also, by EEC definition, what we used to call table wine, i.e. one that has less than 15° alcohol and is meant to be drunk with a meal, as opposed to the *heavy* wines Sherry, Port, Vermouth, etc.

liquorice some people smell this in mature Nebbiolo.

lively a wine that seems bursting with *fruit* and flavour; often due to a very slight 'prickle' of carbon dioxide in the wine, which may for this reason be left intentionally by its maker.

long a wine with good *length*, or a good *finish*, is long.

macération carbonique French for *carbonic maceration*.

maderized sometimes used instead of *oxidized* for a white wine, especially when it's meant without malice – e.g. for a fortified wine such as Madeira (from which the name derives) or for a very old wine that is still interesting despite slight oxidation.

maturity that period in a wine's development after its youth and before it starts to decline. It can be after three years or after three decades, depending on the wine. 'Mature' is a complimentary term, as opposed to 'old' or 'faded', which are criticisms.

meaty substantial and *full bodied* in flavour, often just as the tannin is starting to reveal the *fruit*.

mercaptan substance formed by hydrogen sulphide (H_2S) that smells like rotten eggs. A fault, and one Australians are very keen on.

minerally* smell of assorted minerals, one that I find suggests volcanic deposits and associate with the Hunter Valley in New South Wales.

minty many people smell this spearmint (not peppermint) flavour in California Cabernets, especially those from the Napa Valley.

Mosel German wine in tallish green bottles, produced in the valley of the Mosel (Moselle in France).

mousey nasty smell associated with bacteriological fault in wine.

mulberries* smell (and colour) I associate with Syrah.

must grape pulp mixture that ferments into wine.

noble adjective used to describe those grape varieties that are most respected and which can produce wines that mature to magnificence. Cabernet Sauvignon, Merlot, Pinot Noir, Syrah, Nebbiolo, Chardonnay, Riesling and Sémillon are the most obvious candidates, but almost all of the grape varieties mentioned in this book apart from Aramon, Carignan, Laski Riesling and Chasselas have some claim to nobility – and there are bottles that prove that even these have some blue blood.

noble rot see *botrytis cinerea*.

nose (v.t. and n.) the nose of a wine is its *bouquet* or *aroma*, depending on its state of *maturity*. It's the flavour you can smell. You nose a wine when you consciously smell it.

oaky a complimentary term meaning that you can smell some attractive wood-derived flavour in the wine (c.f. *woody*).

oxidized wine that has been exposed to air for too long and has become stale and flat. A criticism of any table, sorry *light*, wine.

peachy* self-explanatory smell I associate with Viognier.

pear drops rather chemical smell reminiscent of acetate or nail-polish remover, sometimes found in youthful Beaujolais.

pencil shavings* the smell (of the wood not the lead) I find in Cabernet Franc.

perfumed wine with lots of smellable flavour, usually of a slightly musky sort. A white wine adjective.

perlant very slightly sparkling, even less so than a wine that is *petillant*.

petillant slightly sparkling, same as *spritz(ig)*.

petit château wine from a single

Bordeaux property that is not officially classified, i.e. not a *cru classé*.

petrol flavour of mature Riesling, especially German.

plummy rich fruitiness particularly associated with mature Merlot.

pourriture noble French for *botrytis cinerea*.

powerful lots of very easy-to-perceive flavour, plus alcohol.

pricked same as *acetic*.

prickle slight sparkle, same as *spritz(ig)*.

racy lively, used often for white wine, especially Riesling.

raspberries characteristic scent of the Pinot Noir. Some find that Zinfandel smells of raspberries too.

residual sweetness amount of sweetness left in the wine after fermentation has been completed.

rich luscious and *full bodied*, though not necessarily very sweet. A rich red wine may taste slightly sweet (not a word often used to describe reds) but probably because of its alcohol content.

rotten eggs smell of *mercaptan* or hydrogen sulphide (H_2S).

short wine with no *length* of flavour.

smoky characteristic of the Chardonnay grape; a broad sort of flavour.

soft wine with too little tannin. So applicable to red wine only.

soupy wine with no distinct flavour, usually low in *acidity* and quite *full bodied*. Old-style Burgundies shipped to Britain were often soupy.

sparkling in Europe, where the lawyers of Champagne have influence, all wine that fizzes, but is not made in the Champagne region, is called sparkling wine.

spicy Gewürztraminer has an exotic floral sort of spice, while some red grapes, notably Merlot, have a fruity sort.

spritz(ig) wines that are slightly sparkling.

steely rather loose term used chiefly for whites such as Sauvignon and very cool-climate Chardonnays, meaning they have lots of *acidity* and a very pure flavour.

still not sparkling.

sulphury wines that have an excess of the much-used disinfectant sulphur dioxide (SO_2) may smell of recently struck matches or coke-fired ovens. The smell can be dissipated by swirling the offending wine around the glass.

supple wine without too much tannin and lots of attractive *fruit*, usually used of fairly youthful reds in which one might not expect such a quality, e.g. *Clarets*.

sweaty saddle famous Australian tasting term, probably what I call *minerally*.

sweet self-explanatory, but rarely used for red wines.

tannic wine containing lots of *tannin*.

tannin preservative that comes from the skins, stalks and pips of grapes (and from wood too) and tastes like cold stewed tea.

tar some people smell this on Nebbiolo wines, others on Syrah. Both grapes have a depth of colour that helps the auto-suggestion along.

tart wine with too much youthful *acidity*. A pejorative term similar to *green*.

thin wine lacking *body*, to the extent of being watery.

tobacco* flavour I associate with Tempranillo (different from cigars and cigar boxes!).

trigger word expression used to trigger off a mental impression of a wine. If I smell Tempranillo, for instance, I say 'tobacco' to myself and can therefore identify it as such. Very useful for blind tasting, and for measuring samples against the acceptable norm.

truffles some tasters find this elusive scent in the Nebbiolo wines of Piedmont, great white truffle country.

vanilla self-explanatory flavour closely associated with American oak, in which almost all red Rioja and many California reds are matured.

vapour my term for the collection of *volatiles* a wine gives off to communicate its flavour to your olfactory receptors, and thence to the brain.

varietal varietal wine (American term) is named after the predominant grape variety from which it was made. This is in contrast to generic wines, named after a wine region and, supposedly, style. Thus there used to be in Britain, and still are in America and Australia, wines labelled Burgundy, Claret and even Sauterne (no *s* on the end) because they were made dimly in the reflection of the region's style.

vegetal wine smelling of assorted vegetative matter. Not quite reminiscent of the hedgerow, as *herbaceous*, but of the vegetable patch. Pinot Noir often has this flavour.

velvety description of texture, usually used for wines with lots of glycerine and not much *tannin*.

vinegary smelling *acetic*.

violets smell some associate with Nebbiolo, others with Pinot Noir.

viscosity ('stickiness') golden syrup is very viscous, water not at all. A viscous wine is full bodied and leaves great trails down the side of the glass after it has been swirled about. Viscosity is a sign of *body*.

vitis vinifera the family of vines that are specifically designed for bearing wine grapes, as opposed to wild vines.

volatile something that's volatile vapourizes easily and gives off lots of volatiles that comprise what I've called a wine's *vapour*, which conveys the flavour of a wine to the olfactory receptors. All wines are volatile to a greater or lesser extent. The warmer they are and the more aromatic the grape varieties from which they were made, the more volatile they will be. A wine is described as volatile if it is in fact too volatile, i.e. it is giving off flavour so readily that it is starting to taste *acetic*.

volatile acidity ('VA') acescence, or the quality of being *acetic*.

weedy* a combination of herbaceous and tart.

weight all wines have one and, just as for people, it's a measure of how much *body* they have.

woody the unacceptable face of oak: a nasty, wet, mouldy sort of flavour that comes (but not often) from a cask in poor condition.

yeasty smell of fermenting yeasts.

yield the amount of wine produced per area of vines. The French measure it in hectolitres per hectare and call it *rendement*. Thirty is low and one hundred high.

Acknowledgements

As anyone writing on the subject would, I owe a great deal to Michael Broadbent's *Wine Tasting* (Christie's and Mitchell Beazley); also to all my generous friends in the wine trade; to Edmund Penning-Rowsell and to Dr John Piggott.

Index

Page numbers in **bold type** refer to the main text entry on a particular topic; page number in *italic* refer to maps.